Teaching with Conf
in Higher Educatio

Presenting higher education teaching as a performative, creative, and improvisational activity, *Teaching with Confidence in Higher Education* explores how skills and techniques from the performing arts can be used to increase the confidence and enhance the performance of teachers. Guiding readers to reflect on their own teaching practices, this helpful and innovative book proposes practical techniques that will improve higher education teachers' abilities to lead and facilitate engaging and interactive learning sessions.

Encouraging the creation of inclusive learning experiences, the book offers insights into how performative techniques can help to place the student centre stage. Drawing on a variety of performing arts contexts, including acting, singing, stand-up comedy, and dance, as well as interviews with academics and performers, the book helps readers to:

- Critically analyse their own practice, identifying areas for improvement
- Manage their anxiety and 'stage fright' when it comes to teaching
- Become more aware of both their voice and body, establishing professional techniques to improve physical and vocal performance
- Learn to improvise in order to prepare for the unprepared
- Understand the concepts of active learning and inclusivity within the classroom.

Raising awareness of good practice as well as potential areas for development, *Teaching with Confidence in Higher Education* is ideal for anyone new to teaching in higher education or looking to improve student engagement through the performance aspects of their teaching.

Richard Bale is a Senior Fellow of the Higher Education Academy (SFHEA) and a Senior Teaching Fellow in Educational Development at the Centre for Higher Education Research and Scholarship, Imperial College London, UK.

Teaching with Confidence in Higher Education

Applying Strategies from the Performing Arts

Richard Bale

Routledge
Taylor & Francis Group

LONDON AND NEW YORK

First published 2020
by Routledge
2 Park Square, Milton Park, Abingdon, Oxon OX14 4RN

and by Routledge
52 Vanderbilt Avenue, New York, NY 10017

Routledge is an imprint of the Taylor & Francis Group, an informa business

British Library Cataloguing-in-Publication Data
A catalogue record for this book is available from the British Library

Library of Congress Cataloguing-in-Publication Data
A catalogue record has been requested for this book

ISBN: 9780367193638 (hbk)
ISBN: 9780367193652 (pbk)
ISBN: 9780429201929 (ebk)

Typeset in Times New Roman
by Cenveo® Publisher Services

Printed and bound by CPI Group (UK) Ltd, Croydon, CR0 4YY

Contents

Illustrations

FIGURES

TABLES

Foreword

Kate Clinton, known in the United States for her work as a political comedian, wrote in her book *Don't Get Me Started* that "teaching is performance art." As a performer who was once a high school English teacher, Clinton understands the value of performing for the purpose of inspiring and engaging students. Her metaphor, which conceptualises the act of teaching as an artistic performance, nicely sums up the main premise behind this book.

I have been pondering the junction between teaching and performance for the past 15 years, when oftentimes I find myself teaching during the day and acting at night. I was first an actor and then a teacher, so like Clinton I soon realised that a confident performance in the classroom has the power to engage students and promote active learning.

It is fair to say that everything I know about teaching I learned in the theatre: from standing with presence in front of the class to using my voice to persuade students, or moving around the classroom with purpose to make specific points. My lesson is my script and I deliver it the same way I would deliver the lines of a play. As a teacher I know what I want from my students, the same way an actor knows what his or her character wants from the other characters.

In this indispensable book, Richard Bale brilliantly explores the convergence of teaching and performance. He walks us through ways of incorporating performance techniques in our teaching. He gives us opportunities to reflect on our own teaching and to examine how performance can play a role in our own pedagogy. Like in an acting class, he walks us through breathing exercises. He guides us in fine-tuning our voices and bodies, which are our most valuable instruments as teachers.

Bale also introduces us to improvisations and shows us their value in developing our presence and agility in the classroom. He shows us how we can contribute to transform our students into active learners. He demonstrates that in Clinton's metaphor of teaching as performance art, students are not simple audience members, but they are performers themselves.

But his book goes beyond a compilation of performance techniques applicable to teaching and offers an array of perspectives on teaching and performance by teachers, practitioners, and artists. These invaluable insights appear throughout the book adding a range of textures, sounds, and colours to the chapters.

As an actor and teacher, I believe it is important that teachers take acting classes, study scenes, and read plays. This training will not only improve their performance and presence in the classroom, but will also develop their empathetic skills. This is because they will be working on understanding the needs and motivations of others. They will be embodying other people, literally putting themselves in somebody else's shoes. By making a clear and practical connection between teaching and performance, Bale's book represents a significant step in the right direction.

Marco Aponte-Moreno
Berkeley, California

Acknowledgements

My grateful thanks go to my Commissioning Editor, Sarah Tuckwell, and to her editorial team at Routledge. I would also like to thank the teachers and performers who agreed to be interviewed for the book, and whose wise contributions appear throughout the chapters. Thanks also to Jesse Stommel, who connected me with some of the interviewees via Twitter.

I have had much encouragement from many colleagues and friends, too numerous to mention here, but their support and insightful discussions have helped me to complete this book. I am very grateful to the students who agreed to be photographed during their micro-teaching session, and to Mary Harrington for her interesting insights into teaching and for her help in finding an image of the brain and the amygdala – reproduced with kind permission of Daniel P. Kennedy, Ralph Adolphs and Elsevier. I am also very thankful for the thoughtful and constructive feedback on chapter drafts provided by Martin Billingham, Megan Bylsma, Clare Chandler, David Jay, Susan Maloney, Anna McNamara, and Mary Seabrook, and to Marco Aponte-Moreno for agreeing to write a Foreword for the book and for his feedback and insights on performance and teaching.

While writing this book, I developed a short course on performative aspects of teaching, which was attended by several graduate teaching assistants where I work and teach at Imperial College London. I am grateful for the stimulating discussions as well as the student feedback received after this course, which helped me to develop some of the ideas in the book.

Finally, thanks as always to David and to my immediate family and close friends for their ongoing support and for the occasional reminders that I had a book to write!

Introduction

If we take some of the basic characteristics associated with performance, such as rehearsing material and delivering content, often live, in front of an audience, it is not so difficult to make a comparison with teaching. Performers might rehearse material before entertaining an audience on a stage, and they will hopefully receive an applause at the end. In a similar vein, teachers prepare material for their students, they might give a lecture on a stage, or they might stimulate discussions between students in a tutorial, and through skills of facilitation and the ability to motivate others, the students leave the class feeling inspired, having made progress in their learning.

There is an important difference between the goals of a teacher and a performer, however. A performer seeks to entertain, perhaps also to provoke or to inspire, but the key goal is to entertain and to hear a rapturous applause from the audience. A teacher, on the other hand, does not, first and foremost, seek to entertain. Instead, a teacher seeks to engage students, which in turn motivates them to take an active role in their learning. These differences in goals aside, the broad similarities between teaching and performance seem to be quite evident. Many teachers I have spoken to have likened the role of a teacher to that of a performer, but this topic is rarely addressed in higher education.

The benefits of applying performing arts techniques in other fields have been discussed in a variety of contexts, such as language learning (e.g. Leaver et al. 2005), leadership (e.g. Aponte-Moreno 2017), management education (e.g. Monks et al. 2001), and in the training of interpreters (e.g. Bale 2016; Bendazzoli 2009). In the primary and secondary education sectors, teacher training often includes courses related to performance, such as use and care of the voice, awareness of body language, and presentation skills. However, it is less common to find such provision for academics teaching in higher education. Nevertheless, there is growing recognition of the need to support academics to develop their teaching performance, with some universities now offering short courses on performative aspects of teaching. There is also some evidence that academics themselves are becoming more aware of students' shifting expectations of their lecturers; for example, Wong and Chiu (2019) found that academics report challenges in navigating their role as an educator and as an entertainer.

The increasing availability of training courses for teachers in higher education is to be welcomed. Much of this training focuses on core issues of teaching techniques and assessment and feedback approaches. This overdue desire to professionalise teaching in higher education lays the foundation to provide a more comprehensive approach to pedagogic training, including a focus on the performative aspects of the teacher's role. With this in mind, this book aims to start conversations about the performance-related skills involved in teaching, and to explore what we, as higher education teachers, might learn from various types of performer, such as actors, singers, and comedians. My aim is not to provide an exhaustive account of all the potential ways in which teaching might be compared with performance; nor is it my aim to list all the possible tips, skills, and techniques that might be learned from performing artists. Instead, I would like to promote critical reflection on the higher education teacher's role, and to encourage consideration of potential ways in which we might draw on the performer's craft in order to increase confidence and enhance performance in the teacher role. All of this has the central goal of enabling teachers to facilitate more engaging, more interactive, and more student-centred learning experiences.

WHO IS THIS BOOK FOR?

This book is aimed at teachers who are relatively new to teaching in higher education, such as early career academics, graduate teaching assistants, and professionals who teach practice-focused courses on an associate basis. However, as mentioned above, the performative aspects of teaching are rarely addressed in higher education pedagogic training courses, so the techniques discussed in the book may also be of interest to more experienced academics. The insights gained here can be applied in the classroom as well as in other professional engagements, such as delivering conference presentations and in research dissemination and public engagement activities.

HOW IS THIS BOOK STRUCTURED?

The book consists of seven chapters, each of which discusses a different aspect of performance. There is a strong practical focus, promoting reflection on individual practice. To help with this, there are regular opportunities to 'pause for reflection', where you are encouraged to relate the content of the chapters to your own practice context. In some chapters, there are suggested exercises drawn from a variety of performing arts contexts, sometimes in adapted form. These exercises serve to illustrate further the links between teaching and performance, and provide examples of some of the techniques you might try in your teaching context. Whilst the emphasis is on practice, there are references to the scholarly literature in order to provide theoretical underpinning for the key concepts of performance and performativity, particularly in Chapter 1.

As part of the research for the book, I gathered insights on teaching and performance from 10 colleagues, all of whom have experience of performance, and most are also teachers in higher education. I gathered responses either in semi-structured interviews or in written questionnaires. The interviewees work in a variety of roles and contexts in the United Kingdom, the United States, Canada, and Australia, so depending on location, time differences, and availability, the interviews were conducted either face to face, on Skype, or interviewees provided written responses to a series of questions. The interview questions served to guide the conversations so that we discussed the main themes in the chapters of the book, but the interviewees were encouraged to talk freely about their experiences, even if their comments did not explicitly address all of the planned questions. The interviews were transcribed and the transcripts can be found in the appendix at the end of the book. The voices of the interviewees are present throughout the chapters in the form of direct quotations from the full interview transcripts. In some places, these quotations appear against a shaded background to signify that they are not integrated as part of the main text, but instead are intended to add additional views in relation to the topics explored throughout the book.

WHO ARE THE INTERVIEWEES?

Sofia Alexiadou – Interview 1

Sofia Alexiadou is a Lecturer in Lighting at the Liverpool Institute for Performing Arts. She is a practising freelance lighting designer in theatres across Europe, having designed lights for more than 90 shows across different genres. She holds a Master's degree in Theatre Studies (Distinction) and is currently a PhD candidate in the same field. Among her latest credits are collaborations with distinguished European artists such as Mariusz Trelinski, Thomas Moschopoulos, and top leading Greek singers Marinella and Haroula Alexiou as well as designs in major opera houses around Europe and the prestigious ancient Greek theatre of Epidaurus. Sofia encourages her students to seek out and experiment with new things and ideas, to follow their interests, and to think "outside the box."

Lindsay Masland – Interview 2

Lindsay Masland is an Associate Professor of Psychology and the Coordinator for Early Career Programs for the Center for Academic Excellence at Appalachian State University in Boone, North Carolina. She received her PhD in School and Educational Psychology with a concentration in Methodology and Statistics from the University of Georgia in 2011. She serves as a Consulting Editor for the journal *Scholarship of Teaching and Learning in Psychology* and is active in Division 2 of the American Psychological Association (Society for the Teaching of Psychology). Lindsay teaches courses in education, psychology, and statistics to future teachers and school psychologists at both the undergraduate and graduate levels. Her research interests lie at the intersection of academic motivation, effective teaching practices, and social justice, and her passion is to help educators make instructional choices that lead to transformative educational experiences for the many types of students they find in their classrooms. Outside of the classroom, Lindsay can be found cooking, mothering, running, tap dancing, crafting, and performing musical theatre.

Kate Nasser – Interview 3

Kate Nasser has always combined intellectual pursuits with her profession of teaching human interaction and organisational behaviour. Concurrently and throughout these many years, she has performed in musical comedies and plays as singer, actor, and dancer. She accounts her professional success to the combination of intellect and performance. In other words, reach them to teach them. Kate Nasser, The People Skills Coach™, is founder and President of CAS, Inc. and author of *Leading Morale*. You can find out more about Kate's work by visiting www.katenasser.com.

David Jay – Interview 4

David Jay is a Tutor, Lecturer, and teacher trainer based in the Cambridge Language Centre at Anglia Ruskin University. His background is in Communicative Language Teaching, and he has over 20 years' experience of teaching and training in a range of contexts, including pre- and in-sessional programmes, teacher development courses, academic skills support, and undergraduate modules in grammar, pragmatics, and sociolinguistics. David's research interests include the evaluation of classroom practice, techniques for classroom management, and the application of communicative methodologies in higher education contexts. He is a graduate of King's College, Cambridge (Modern Languages) and a Fellow of the Higher Education Academy.

Susan Maloney – Interview 5

Susan Maloney is a casual Tutor and Lecturer in the School of Law, Humanities and the Arts at the University of Wollongong. Her career began in advertising. She then studied at the University of Wollongong before transferring to UC Santa Cruz, where she also taught film and video. Before returning to teaching, Susan worked in video production in California. She now teaches communications and media at the University of Wollongong. Her academic interests include film, television, urban design and architectural innovation, street art, surveillance, and the relationship between media use and identity. She has been involved in research projects focused on optimising and improving pedagogical practice. Susan has studied various dance forms and is interested in the retention of Pacific Island dance and culture.

Martin Billingham – Interview 6

Martin Billingham is an academic, an educator, and a stand-up comedian with a specialism in the connection between teaching and stand-up comedy performance. He is currently at the Institute of Education, UCL working on the assessment of effective communication within the classroom, specialising in oracy, dialogic learning, and group work. Martin's long-term goal is to complete a PhD study on the impact of stand-up comedy training with early career teachers. The intent is to build a rigorous and informed method for use in conjunction with Initial Teacher Training. You can find out more about Martin's work by visiting https://www.listen-learn-standup-speak.com/.

James Marples – Interview 7

James Marples is an Australian songwriter, composer, and performer. His composition work for contemporary dance and theatre has been performed at Sadlers Wells, Southbank Centre and Southwark Playhouse, UK. He has released records on a number of UK independent record labels and received BBC radio play. As a bandleader, for 12 years he fronted the Milkshakers, a 1950s rock n roll band that performed throughout the UK and Europe. In 2018, he was the artist in residence at the Menzies Centre for Australian Studies at King's College London, and received Arts Council funding for his project 'Colonial Sun' exploring Australian national identity through songwriting. In 2019, he performed an eight-night run of 'Twelvis', a live art concert and performance lecture about Elvis Presley.

Megan Bylsma – Interview 8

Megan Bylsma is an Art and Animation History instructor at Red Deer College, in Red Deer, Alberta, Canada. While Art and Animation History are her classroom topics and rank high in her top ten favourite things to talk about, her passion is in her belief that relationship-based, student-focused learning is one of the most effective teaching approaches on the planet. She attended Red Deer College and the University of Lethbridge for her BFA – Art History/Museum Studies before attending Queen's University for her MA – focusing on mid-20th century Canadian Art History.

Anna McNamara – Interview 9

Anna McNamara is Director of Learning and Teaching at the Guildford School of Acting, University of Surrey. She trained in Musical Theatre at the Guildford School of Acting before moving into teaching full time in 2001, gaining an MA in Education. Anna holds teaching qualifications in dance (ISTD), singing and music (Trinity College London), and drama (QTS). A qualified first aider and a qualified mental health first aider, Anna is a Senior Fellow of the Higher

Education Academy and a Fellow of the Royal Society of Arts. She is currently researching a PhD in Actor Training Pedagogy. In 2017, she was awarded the University of Surrey Vice Chancellor's award for Teacher of the Year.

Clare Chandler – Interview 10

Clare Chandler is Senior Lecturer in Musical Theatre at the University of Wolverhampton. She teaches a variety of topics across musical theatre practice, such as acting technique, vocal technique, critical analysis, and engagement with critical theory. Clare has varied experience as a performer: she has worked as a singer, as an actress, and a musician in a variety of different genres. Clare's research interests include the impact of technology on the development of contemporary musical theatre, feminism and musical theatre, and pedagogical practice and performer training. Clare has an MA in Musical Theatre from Goldsmiths University. She has worked as a dramaturg on *Em,* a new musical by Benjamin Till, and recently directed the national premiere of *Angry Birds the Musical* by Dougal Irvine. She is currently developing a new musical called *Brecht's Threepenny Bits* – deconstructing the idea of the singular theatrical Marxist genius with his harem of lovers! Clare is a member of the Musical Theatre Network and co-chair of the New Researchers' Network Committee.

SUBSEQUENT CHAPTERS

The following chapters focus on various aspects of performance and suggest techniques and exercises that can be used to improve performance and increase confidence. In **Chapter 1**, we explore the idea of teaching as a performative act and discuss the links between teaching and performance. **Chapter 2** enables you to reflect on your teaching style and to identify aspects of good practice and areas for development in your teaching. Here, we discuss **microteaching** and **peer observation** as two possible tools to enable you to conduct an initial assessment of your teaching. We then look in **Chapter 3** at the nature of performance anxiety and stage fright, and suggest some exercises used by performers to manage nerves and anxiety.

 Chapter 4 focuses on the **voice** and **breathing**, drawing on techniques used by singers and other performers to ensure that the voice remains robust and healthy. **Chapter 5** shifts the focus onto the **body**, drawing on insights from various actor training techniques. **Chapter 6** looks at the anxieties that teachers experience about **unpreparedness**, taking inspiration from performing artists, particularly in relation to **improvisation.**

Finally, **Chapter 7** discusses the concept of **active learning,** and how this shifts the focus away from the teacher as the sole 'performer' in the classroom. Here, we also discuss the important issue of **inclusivity** in higher education, highlighting that a performative approach to learning and teaching can promote greater inclusion, participation, and collaboration.

REFERENCES

Aponte-Moreno, M. (2017) Writing and enacting ethical dilemmas: Using drama to foster responsible leadership behavior. *Journal of Leadership Studies* 11(2), 69–71.

Bale, R. (2016) Online to on stage: Towards a performative approach to interpreter education. *Scenario* 10(2), 8–21.

Bendazzoli, C. (2009) Theatre and creativity in interpreter training. In Fernández García, M. I., Zucchiatti, M., & M. G. Biscu (eds.) *L'esperienza teatrale nella formazione dei futuri mediatori linguistici e culturali.* Bologna: BUP, 153–164.

Leaver, B. L, Ehrman, M., & Shekhtman, B. (2005) *Achieving Success in Second Language Acquisition.* Cambridge: CUP.

Monks, K., Barker, P., & Ní Mhanacháin, A. (2001) Drama as an opportunity for learning and development. *Journal of Management Development* 20(5), 414–423.

Wong, B., & Chiu, Y-L. T. (2019) Let me entertain you: The ambivalent role of university lecturers as educators and performers. *Educational Review* 71(2), 218–233.

Chapter 1

Teaching and performance

"The lecture is the obvious format that highlights the link between teaching and performance. We just have to think about the lecture hall as an auditorium. There is an oratory tradition to these spaces, but the Greeks referred to the stage as the orchestra, which means the dancing place. Nowadays, lectures also add a huge screen and project presentation slides, so our students are sitting in a kind of cinema. This can, perhaps inevitably, build a sense of expectation of the lecturer to fulfil the role of performer."

Anna McNamara, Interview 9

When we are teaching, to some extent we have probably all had the feeling that we are performing; that we are 'playing a role'; that we are 'on stage'; that we are acting a part. However, I would like to say from the outset that I do not view teachers as *actors*: this perspective places the teacher centre stage, which is unhelpful in a higher education landscape where we are focusing more and more on student-centred approaches and active learning (see Chapter 7). It is also clear that teachers are not actors; they are themselves, perhaps variations of themselves, but themselves nonetheless. I return to this point below.

A current trend in higher education in many countries is the shifting relationship between students and their universities. This is driven by the increasing marketisation of higher education, from the emergence of for-profit colleges in the United States (e.g. Angulo 2016) to increasing tuition fees in the United Kingdom. All of this leads to greater consumeristic expectations of students. For example, a Universities UK survey (2017) of just over 1,000 undergraduates revealed that almost half of students (47%) considered themselves to be customers of their universities. This in turn has implications for the professionalisation of teaching in higher education and the subsequent scrutiny of teaching quality and teaching performance. Here, we are not concerned with performance in terms of quality management, and review and evaluation of teachers' performance. Instead, we focus on the teacher's own notions of performance, mindful of the potential for teachers to experience greater (performance) anxiety as a result of the increased focus on teaching quality and consumeristic relationships with students.

Many aspects of life can be and have been explored through a performance lens, and it has been argued for many decades that our everyday interactions have aspects of a theatrical performance. Specifically in the higher education teaching context, the academic and performer Lee Campbell (2019) has written about the role of performance in pedagogy, culminating in the publication of an edited volume on critical performative pedagogy. Zooming out from higher education, the renowned sociologist Erving Goffman devised the concept of dramaturgical analysis. He observed that people 'behave', or 'act', differently in different situations, and with different people, preserving a private presentation of self for the backstage space. Goffman (1956) outlined his ideas in his first book, *The Presentation of Self in Everyday Life*. In this chapter, we start from this premise that we present ourselves in different ways in different social contexts, and we look specifically at the teaching context. We will explore some of the key terms used throughout the book and attempt to define concepts which are relevant when considering performance aspects of a teacher's role.

TEACHING *AS* PERFORMANCE OR TEACHING *IS* PERFORMANCE?

> Teaching is about reaching people with your subject. Performance is about reaching people with your message.
>
> Kate Nasser, Interview 3

In discussing teaching and performance, it is important to clarify precisely how we consider teaching and performance to be related: do we say teaching *is* (a) performance or do we just describe teaching *as* performance? What is the difference? As is evident by the topic of this book, we often tend to refer to almost anything as being a performance. A famous example is the quote from Shakespeare's *As You Like It*, in which Jacques begins a monologue with "All the world's a stage," characterising life as a play being performed by us, the actors. However, McAuley (2010) cautions against considering an ever-increasing number of scenarios and contexts to *be* performances. As Schechner (2013) points out, an important factor in determining whether something is deemed to be a performance is what cultural, social, and historical conventions count as performance. This means that what *is* performance is not static but changes over time and from culture to culture, and lines between what is performance and what is an everyday activity often become blurred. A contemporary example is the fast-paced and often dramatic world of politics: at the time of writing, the highest political office, the US President, is currently occupied by a former reality TV star.

It is unlikely that current social or cultural conventions, anywhere in the world, would categorise teaching as *being* performance. However, anything has the potential to be viewed *as* performance. Schechner (2013: 41) gives the example of maps as performance, explaining that, in their various forms, maps perform certain functions, such as depicting clear, but artificial, boundaries between nation states, or portraying the northern hemisphere with relatively bigger territories as compared to land masses in the southern hemisphere, showing the world from the preferred viewpoint of the colonial powers. Schechner concludes that *as* provides a useful way of viewing a particular topic through the lens of something else, without committing to a firm comparison between the two.

> What the 'as' says is that the object of study will be regarded 'from the perspective of', 'in terms of', 'interrogated by' a particular discipline of study.
>
> (Schechner 2013: 42)

This is what is at the heart of this book: encouraging reflection on our teaching practice and performance; considering teaching *from the perspective of* performing arts; *in terms of* skills and techniques used by performers; *interrogated by* performance studies, all of which designate teaching as having elements of performance without describing the teacher inherently as a performer, an actor, or a sage-on-the-stage character.

WHAT IS PERFORMANCE?

Returning to the point above about marketisation and consumerisation of higher education, the notion of performance draws our attention to standards, success, and potential consequences for substandard performance. In the arts, performance is about entertaining (an audience) and pursuing a creative endeavour. However, neither of these concepts of performance captures the essence of performance from the perspective of a teacher. The influential performance theorist and theatre director Richard Schechner (2003: 8) identifies several characteristics which are unique to performance, namely demonstration or showing of skills or talents, audience members, ordering of time sequences, and a high degree of self-awareness on the part of the performer. It is possible to see how this idea of performance can be used to frame a teacher's performance. Teachers simultaneously demonstrate their own skills of presentation, explanation, and so on, but they also guide their 'audience' – their students – to learn new skills and to gain new knowledge. For any teacher who has planned a class, it is also apparent that time is never your friend, and it is important to consider carefully how long the different segments of the lesson will take, and how these interrelate. Finally, as teachers, we are encouraged to be reflective practitioners, casting a critical eye over our own practice both during class and afterwards in order to reflect-in-action and to reflect-on-action (Schön 1983) (see Chapter 2). This means we have a high degree of self-awareness.

In terms of the extent of performance and where it might arise, Schechner (2013: 31) identifies eight situations in which performances might occur:

1   in everyday life – cooking, socialising, 'just living'
2   in the arts
3   in sports and other popular entertainments
4   in business
5   in technology
6   in sex
7   in ritual – sacred and secular
8   in play

Schechner acknowledges that this list is by no means exhaustive, and that many of the situations overlap and form integral parts of each other. He uses this list simply to highlight that performance is a ubiquitous construct, found everywhere, but that it is also difficult to define or to determine its limits and boundaries. For Fleming (2016), what distinguishes performance from everyday life (number 1 in Schechner's list of situations) is the emphasis on reflection and awareness of self during the activity, in our case teaching. This means that we can move away from the more obvious notions of performance, such as standing on a stage and speaking in front of an audience, and focus instead on the self-awareness, self-reflection, and, in some ways, the vulnerabilities of the teacher. This, in essence, is where teaching meets performance.

WHAT DOES IT MEAN TO PERFORM?

As we have seen from Schechner's depiction of performance above, the act of performing occurs in a variety of ways, from the obvious performance on stage or screen, to performing roles at ceremonies or social events, to navigating performances in everyday life, such as performing a job role in the workplace. We are usually quite aware when we are performing, and we can quite easily spot the difference between 'being ourselves' and 'playing a role'. Or is this always the case, particularly in the workplace, and even more specifically, in teaching?

PAUSE FOR REFLECTION:

Think about how you are as a person in everyday life and how you are when you are teaching? How do you think your friends and family would view you if they saw you in a teaching context? Would they find your everyday 'persona' different from your teaching 'persona'? Do *you* think you have a teaching (performing) persona?

The questions above aim to provoke reflection about who you are when you are 'just being you' – if such a thing even exists – and who you are when you are *performing the role* of a teacher. Friends and family members, who know me solely in a social, non-working/teaching context, have often remarked that they find the idea of me 'standing in front of a class' funny, interesting, intriguing, strange – and other adjectives of choice. What I take from this is that they are used to seeing me (perform) in a particular context – everyday life – and so they find the idea of me performing the role of a teacher, which they know well from their own experiences of being taught themselves, funny, interesting, etc. In short, for them at least, when I am teaching, I am a version of myself which is unfamiliar to them. When I reverse these questions

13

and think about some of my friends and family in their workplace roles, I have similar thoughts about them, too.

> Learning spaces are far from stoic, quiet halls they may have once been. Academics compete for attention with the laptops and devices that students use. I feel that when I stand at the front of a lecture hall or move my way through tutorials, I have to be 'on' and provide as flawless a performance as possible. Our lectures are now recorded for playback, they aren't ephemeral, they are packaged performance pieces. Essentially they double as video on-demand.
>
> Susan Maloney, Interview 5

This notion of different personas brings us to the idea of *acting*. If we are performing a role in the classroom, to what extent are we acting? I said from the outset that I do not consider teaching to be acting, as the teacher is always herself or himself, though as we have seen, s/he may be a slightly different version of herself or himself. Acting, and the reason teaching should not be considered to belong to this type of performance, is illustrated succinctly by actor and performance theorist, Michael Kirby:

> To act means to *feign*, to simulate, to represent, to *impersonate*. [...] In a performance, we usually know when a person is acting and when he is not. [...] There are numerous performances that do not use acting.
>
> (Kirby 1972: 3, emphasis added)

The words 'feign' and 'impersonate' in Kirby's definition stand out as clearly not belonging to the role of a teacher. When we teach, we are not playing a character; we are not pretending, feigning, or impersonating. Just as important, however, is Kirby's statement that not all performances include acting: we can perform without acting, without pretending. This is what we do when we teach. Some actors and teachers would disagree with Kirby's emphasis on feigning and pretending, however. In the Meisner technique (see Chapter 6), for example, developed by renowned actor and acting teacher, Sanford Meisner, the focus is on enabling actors "to live truthfully under imaginary circumstances" (Silverberg 1994: 9). In some ways, Meisner's view of acting might be considered to be closer to the role of a teacher, who is practising truthfully and authentically. Nevertheless, the fundamental difference remains: an actor is playing the role of somebody else; a teacher is playing (a version of) herself or himself.

Returning to Kirby's definition of acting – that we *know* when a person is acting – the same might not be said of performing in everyday life. In certain situations, we might change how we behave in order to achieve particular outcomes, and these changes might not be perceptible to others, or even to ourselves. An example from Schechner (2013: 207) is a child raising the pitch of her or his voice to ask for an ice cream, presumably because the child has learned that raised pitch is a common way of asking (politely) for something. Schechner highlights other everyday performances which are marked by the 'performer's' clothes, tone of voice, professional vocabulary, and so on. Again, these performances are subtle, and the person may not be perceived to be performing. However, factors, such as clothing, specific vocabulary, tone of voice, and so on, have a *performative* effect, helping the person to perform their role in the given context, at the given time, in front of the given *audience*.

PAUSE FOR REFLECTION:

Think about what you wear when you are teaching and how you speak; the vocabulary you use; your tone of voice. To what extent is any of this different to how you dress, speak, and present yourself in everyday life?

PERFORMATIVITY

We have used the word 'performative' in relation to teaching several times in this chapter, but this term is somewhat elusive, with a variety of definitions and uses having emerged. The term 'performative' was first coined by philosopher of language, J. L. Austin in 1955. Austin derived the term from 'perform' in relation to utterances, which was later developed further by a student of Austin, John R. Searle, in what he termed *speech acts* (Searle 1969). Austin put forward the idea that certain utterances are not simply descriptions of actions; the utterances themselves *are* actions. An example often used to illustrate this is:

I do (take this woman to be my lawful wedded wife).

In uttering this statement, the speaker is performing an action – in this case, entering into a marriage. This does not mean that words themselves automatically denote actions, however:

> Now at this point one might protest, perhaps even with some alarm, that I seem to be suggesting that marrying is simply saying a few words, that just saying a few words is marrying. Well, that certainly is not the case. The words have to be said in the appropriate circumstances.
>
> (Austin 1979: 235)

This is an important point in Austin's concept of performativity: that performative utterances can denote actions, but that these utterances – and associated performance of actions – must be uttered in a corresponding, appropriate context. At this point, we turn our attention to how performativity relates to teaching and learning.

Interest in performative approaches to learning and teaching has been growing in recent years. In the field of foreign language teaching, for example, the peer-reviewed journal *Scenario* was established in 2007, publishing research dedicated solely to performative teaching, learning, and research, focusing in particular on the role played by drama and theatre in foreign language learning. As Schewe writes:

> It is therefore proposed that 'performative' be used as an umbrella term to describe the (various culturally-specific) forms of foreign language teaching that derive from the performing arts.
>
> (Schewe 2013: 18)

For our purposes, we can extend Schewe's definition to learning and teaching in general. Indeed, Even and Schewe (2016: 182) note that "Performative teaching and learning means that the performative arts, particularly the art of theatre, become a central point of reference." The authors make this statement in relation to the pedagogical activities used to facilitate students' learning, but we can also expand this to incorporate the teacher's own use of skills and techniques from the performing arts to increase her or his confidence as a teacher and to enhance performance in this role. In an even looser sense, we might draw on one of Schechner's interpretations of performativity: "something that is 'like a performance' without actually being a performance in the orthodox or formal sense" (Schechner 2013: 123).

TEACHING AS AN ARTISTIC AND AN AESTHETIC ACTIVITY

The debate around whether teaching is a science or an art is centuries old, but the truth is probably not at one end of a binary scale. However, if we accept the similarities between teaching and performance, as outlined above, it is easy to argue that teaching is an artistic endeavour. Some characterise teaching quite firmly as an art form, and Dawe (1984) goes even further and describes teaching as a performing art. Along with others, such as Eisner (2002), Dawe proposes training which enables teachers to learn experientially – similar to the *actor's studio* – where teachers can practise their teaching techniques, gain critical, constructive feedback, and reflect on their practice. In some ways, lesson observations and microteaching go some way to providing a type of *teacher's studio*, offering experiential training for teachers to practise performing their role as teacher. This is discussed further in Chapter 2.

The emeritus professor of education, Mike Fleming, provides a helpful distinction between two opposing views of art and aesthetics: at one end of the spectrum, we can view artistic endeavours and aesthetic experiences as separate from life itself, so that the artistic object can be analysed in isolation; at the other end, we can consider art to be inextricably linked to life and to the artist who created the piece of work. This is represented by the view of art *is* life. However, Fleming cautions against viewing education at either extreme end of this spectrum.

> Art simplifies in order to explore complexity. The aesthetic dimensions of experience with art should not serve to separate art from life but rather strengthen its ability to enhance perception and intensify experience.
>
> (Fleming 2016:200)

Much of the writings on arts and aesthetics in teaching and learning focus on learning through artistic and aesthetic experiences – often referred to as arts in education – and also discussing what constitutes art, where the boundaries lie between art, aesthetics, and culture (e.g. Fleming 2012). However, this is less relevant for our purposes, as we are focusing on the teacher's role and the extent to which it is helpful to consider our teaching *performance* to be an artistic endeavour. I would argue that Fleming's quote above provides a neat response to this question: in its most basic form, teaching is about breaking complex concepts (or at least, for the learner, concepts, and content which are currently unfamiliar) down into more manageable, simplified chunks, while also drawing links between the topic of study and the learners' experiences and life beyond the classroom. This creative process of simplification and helping learners to relate the content to their own experience echoes Fleming's notion of what constitutes art.

In a theatrical context, the renowned theoretician in performance studies Erika Fischer-Lichte (2008) introduced the concept of an auto-poietic feedback loop. Fischer-Lichte's concept refers to the connections between audience members and performers, on an emotional level, in an ongoing feedback loop. The spectators are engaging with various aspects of the performers' body language, facial expressions, tone of voice, the performance space, and the underlying messages of the performance. The events that unfold, including the aesthetics of, for example, the stage and the performers' and audience members' facial expressions, are dynamic. In the same way, teaching has a similar feedback loop between teacher and students.

> Also in terms of Fischer-Lichte and this notion of autopoiesis, so this cycle of energy and engagement is something that's present within the classroom or the lecture in that there's this cycle of energy and knowledge between the student and the teacher. And as such, as the teacher or the performer, you need to be conscious of that engagement. You're presenting knowledge in a performative manner in order to facilitate understanding. So your teaching, your performance, your practice needs to be reactive and responsive to what's happening in the room. We've all had sessions where you've planned it, you go in and think it's going to be amazing, but for whatever reasons it isn't working and you have to change and adapt in order to meet the audience or get them to meet you. So this relationship between student and teacher is integral to ideas that link teaching and performance.
>
> Clare Chandler, Interview 10

Accepting that teaching has an artistic dimension, Crutchfield poses important questions about the nature of teaching-as-art. He asks what kind of art teaching might be considered to be, ultimately agreeing with Dawe that teaching is a *performing* art. He then goes on to ask about the (artistic) training requirements of teachers, inviting us to reflect on the performance skills which ought to be honed by aspiring teachers (Crutchfield 2015: 104). This is the concern of the following chapters of this book, where we focus on a variety of aspects of performance and discuss how various performing arts techniques might be applied to our roles as teachers.

DRAMA-BASED PEDAGOGY

As Schewe (2013) points out, the use of dramatic art in education has a long history, both in terms of enabling students to learn through drama-based activities, such as acting out scenes, playing a role, and so on, and also in terms of drama as a subject of study in its own right. As mentioned at the start of this chapter, in higher education we are focusing more and more on student-centred approaches in our teaching and encouraging learners to be active participants in, rather than passive recipients of, their learning. This is in keeping with drama-based pedagogy, which engages students using dramatic techniques from drama and theatre. There is a more holistic focus on the learner as a whole, dynamic person, as explained by Dawson and Lee (2018: 17): "Drama-based pedagogy uses strategies that bring together the body and mind through the art of drama/theatre."

The idea of bringing together mind and body is interesting, and leads us to consider how movement, drama, and activity are connected to the brain when learning and teaching are taking place. New insights from neuroscience are starting to shed light not only on learning in general, but also on how drama-based activities can help to stimulate the brain and enhance learning. A particularly interesting interdisciplinary study was conducted by Kiefer et al. (2007), which combined neuroscience with (movement-based) learning, and the findings have interesting implications for the use of techniques which activate both mind and body during learning and teaching.

Kiefer et al. aimed to investigate what was happening in the brain during learning under different conditions. The researchers invented sixty-four objects, so-called *nobjects*, which ensured that research participants had no preconceived notions of the 'objects'. The participants were divided into two groups: members of the experimental group were asked to memorise the names of the nobjects while performing matching movements and gestures. Participants in the control group were asked to memorise the nobjects without any corresponding movements. After learning the names of the nobjects, participants in both groups sat a test. Participants who had learned the nobjects with corresponding movements scored higher than participants in the control group. The higher scores were apparent in terms of accuracy and speed of recall as well as the participants' ability to use the new terms, the nobjects, for their own purposes. The researchers also tracked participants' brain activity using an EEG and found that those in the experimental group had increased activity in the motor regions of the brain. From this, Kiefer et al. concluded that combining movement with learning (positively) impacts on how the brain processes and stores new information.

Since this research, there have been several studies which have translated this neuroscientific work to the classroom. For example, Sambanis (2014) conducted a similar study to the nobject methodology with very positive results. Sambanis calls her technique *scenic learning* which, like the nobject procedure, involves students learning new knowledge in combination with movements, mime, and gestures. She found that students in the experimental group, who had combined learning with movements, performed better on a subsequent recall test when compared with students in the control group. Even more striking, however, were the students' test scores after several weeks: the students in the control group had significantly greater retention of the new knowledge over a longer period of time as compared to the control group.

As well as the findings from studies on movement-based learning, there are also interesting insights into the effects of emotions on learning (Cavanagh 2016). Sambanis (2016) explains that, from functional magnetic resonance imaging (fMRI), we know that positive and negative emotions cause different brain activity, and numerous studies show that we learn better when we are experiencing positive emotions. This is due to a part of the limbic system called the amygdala (See Figure 1.1). The amygdala is essentially the brain's early warning system, which sends messages to other parts of the brain to trigger reactions when certain emotions are activated, for example experiencing fear may trigger a flight response and the person may want to run away from the situation.

Sambanis (2016) explains that knowledge is stored along with the emotions that we associate with our experience of learning that new knowledge. So, if the learning experience invoked negative emotions and was unpleasant, our brain is less likely to reactivate, and therefore recall, this knowledge and is likely to eventually forget this information. Sambanis summarises this as follows:

> In a positive state of mind, we experience learning as enjoyable and rewarding. Based on this, it makes sense to discuss ways to stimulate and foster positive emotions in instructional settings, ways to make teaching moving, both emotionally and physically. Drama in education is one such method.
>
> (Sambanis 2016: 216)

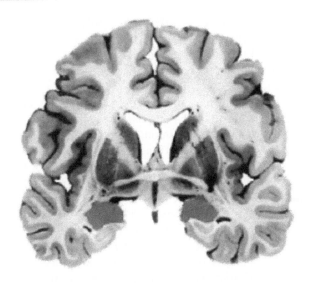

This very brief look at drama and movement-based pedagogy shows that there is potential for positive learning outcomes for students when learning using a variety of active, dramatic techniques. However, I would also argue that these findings can be transferred to the teacher's own context. Particularly if the teacher is feeling nervous or anxious, it would be beneficial to generate positive emotions about the act of teaching, whether this is done by teaching using drama-based methods or using skills and techniques from the performing arts to overcome nerves related to teaching, or a combination of the two.

COMMON ANXIETIES EXPERIENCED BY NEW TEACHERS

When discussing performance and performativity in higher education teaching, we cannot ignore the potential (performance) anxieties experienced by teachers (see Chapter 3). Until relatively recently, teachers in higher education received little or no professional training before beginning their teaching duties (Fish & Fraser 2001), and this only added to academics' anxieties about their roles as teachers. Thankfully, this is now changing in many countries, with faculty members being offered training in learning and teaching leading to formal qualifications, such as postgraduate certificates, diplomas, and master's degrees in education.

Nevertheless, the role of an academic is still highly complex and brings with it a multitude of potential stress factors. There is some research on stress and anxiety among university faculty members, for example a large-scale survey of UK academics in 2006 showed that faculty members' stress levels often increase over time as they try to juggle competing demands on their time in the areas of research, teaching, and administration (Kinman et al. 2006). Linked to this is Kinchin et al.'s (2016) concept of pedagogic frailty, which refers to the situation teachers might finds themselves in when trying to respond to the multiple and changing pressures of the academic role (see also Kinchin & Winstone 2017). There is also research on teaching anxiety, linked, for example, to the personality of the teacher (e.g. Houlihan et al. 2009). There is little research, however, on teaching anxiety explicitly linked to *performance*, particularly in relation to new teachers. This is not to say that teachers do not experience anxiety about their performance before, during, and after class. The idea for this book arose precisely because of the experiences I hear about from colleagues as well as the teaching anxieties that I have experienced myself. In my daily interactions with colleagues, particularly those who are new to teaching, I hear a variety of frequently mentioned anxieties about teaching. I hear about colleagues' experiences during informal conversations and in formal teacher training sessions. These anxieties generally fall into three main categories: preparation and rehearsal, communication, and confidence and identity – summarised in Table 1.1.

Each anxiety in Table 1.1 is about the teacher's performance in the role of the teacher, and many of these might be addressed using techniques of performing artists. We will come back to some of these anxieties in subsequent chapters and discuss how performance skills and exercises can be employed to mitigate the effects of teaching anxiety and help to improve your confidence as a teacher.

PAUSE FOR REFLECTION:

Do you recognise any of the anxieties in Table 1.1? Have you experienced any of them yourself? Are there any anxieties you have which are not mentioned here?

TABLE 1.1 Common teaching anxieties

Preparation and Rehearsal	Communication	Confidence and Identity
Time needed for preparation ('rehearsal')	Competence in English expression	Lack of confidence; fear of speaking in front of a group
Not knowing the answer to students' questions	Accent in English (from teachers who speak English both as their first language and from those who speak English as an additional language)	Lack of identity as a teacher; too close in age to the students
Dealing with unexpected questions	Clarity of explanations	Assertiveness and keeping students' attention
Balance between teaching preparation and research	Communicating clear expectations and dealing with disruptive students	Not being 'good enough' and negatively affecting students' learning

IN SUMMARY

A great teacher reads the crowd, knows when to get quiet and draw them, or get loud and get them up and out of their seats. They know when to move towards a noisy table and use their presence as the reminder to pay attention, and when to flail their arms and make horrendous noises as part of their story-lecture to snap that attention back. I think that a teacher who doesn't know that teaching is a performance probably wonders why they aren't an impactful teacher.

Megan Bylsma, Interview 8

In this chapter, I have drawn comparisons between teaching and performance, describing teaching *as* performance, with performance-like qualities. In particular, drawing on insights from performance studies and performance theory, it is possible to identify certain characteristics of teaching which highlight aspects of performance, namely: the self-awareness, self-reflection, and vulnerability of the teacher in front of an 'audience'. However, although teaching shares many characteristics with performance, it is not the same as acting. When we are teaching, we are not pretending, feigning, or impersonating; we are being ourselves, perhaps a version of ourselves, but ourselves nonetheless.

We also looked at the notion of *performativity*, which has its origins in linguistics and philosophy of language. In educational terms, performative teaching and learning is often used to describe teaching methods which draw on the performing arts. For our purposes, we extend this definition to our practice as teachers and ask how we can make use of techniques and skills from the performing arts in order to improve our teaching performance and increase our confidence as teachers. Drama-based pedagogy is already used in several disciplines at every level of education, from primary to tertiary, and it is possible to see how drama-based techniques can also be of benefit to teachers themselves.

As we know from our own teaching practice, new faculty members often experience anxieties about their role and identity as teachers. The rest of this book discusses how viewing teaching as a performative act, using techniques from the performing arts, can help to allay these performance anxieties and increase teachers' confidence.

REFERENCES AND FURTHER READING

Angulo, A. J. (2016) *Diploma mills: How for-profit colleges stiffed students, tax-payers, and the American dream.* Maryland: John Hopkins University Press.

Austin, J. L. (1979) *How to do things with words*, 3rd ed. Oxford: Oxford University Press. Available at: http://www.oxfordscholarship.com/view/10.1093/019283021X.001.0001/acprof-9780192830210-chapter-10 (accessed 17.10.19).

Campbell, L. (ed.) (2019) *Leap into action: Critical performative pedagogies in art and design education.* New York: Peter Lang.

Cavanagh, S. R. (2016) *The spark of learning: Energizing the college classroom with the science of emotion.* Morgantown, WV: West Virginia University Press.

Crutchfield, J. (2015) Fear and trembling: The role of 'Negative' emotions in a performative pedagogy. *Scenario* 9(2), 101–114.

Dawe, H. (1984) Teaching: A performing art. *The Phi Delta Kappan* 65(8), 548–552.

Dawson, K. & Lee, B. K. (2018) *Drama-based pedagogy: Activating learning across the curriculum.* Bristol: Intellect.

Eisner, E. (2002) *The arts and the creation of mind.* New Haven & London: Yale University Press.

Even, S. & Schewe, M. (2016) Performative teaching, learning research: Introduction. In: Even, S. & Schewe, M. (eds.) *Performatives Lehren, Lernen, Forschen. Performative Teaching, Learning, Research.* Berlin: Schibri, 174–188.

Fischer-Lichte, E. (2008) *The transformative power of performance: A new aesthetic.* London: Routledge.

Fish, T. & Fraser, I. (2001) Exposing the Iceberg of Teaching Anxiety: A Survey of Faculty at Three New Brunswick Universities. *Perspectives: Electronic Journal of the American Association of Behavioral and Social Sciences* 4. Available at: https://sites.google.com/a/aabss.net/american-association-of-behavioral-and-social-sciences—index/home/perspectives-2001 (accessed 17.10.19).

Fleming, M. (2012) *The arts in education: An introduction to aesthetics, theory and pedagogy.* Oxford: Routledge.

Fleming, M. (2016) Exploring the concept of performative teaching and learning. In: Even, S. & Schewe, M. (eds.) *Performatives Lehren, Lernen, Forschen. Performative teaching, learning, research.* Berlin: Schibri, 189–205.

Goffman, E. (1956) *The presentation of self in everyday life.* Edinburgh: University of Edinburgh Social Sciences Research Centre. Available at: https://monoskop.org/images/1/19/Goffman_Erving_The_Presentation_of_Self_in_Everyday_Life.pdf (accessed 17.10.19).

Houlihan, M., Fraser, I., Fenwick, K. D., Fish, T., & Moeller, C. (2009) Personality effects on teaching anxiety and teaching strategies in university professors. *Canadian Journal of Higher Education* 39(1), 61–72.

Kiefer, M., Sim, E-J., Liebich, S., Hauk, O., & Tanaka, J. (2007) Experience-dependent plasticity of conceptual representations in human sensory-motor areas. *Journal of Cognitive Neuroscience* 19(3), 525–542.

Kinchin, I. M. & Winstone, N. E. (eds.) (2017) *Pedagogic frailty and resilience in the university.* Rotterdam: Sense.

Kinchin, I. M., Alpay, E., Curtis, K., Franklin, J., Rivers, C., & Winstone, N. E. (2016) Charting the elements of pedagogic frailty. *Educational Research* 50(1), 1–23.

Kinman, G., Jones, F., & Kinman, R. (2006) The well-being of the UK academy, 1998–2004. *Quality in Higher Education* 12(1), 15–27.

Kirby, M. (1972) On acting and not-acting. *The Drama Review: TDR* 16(1), 3–15.

McAuley, G. (2010) Interdisciplinary field or emerging discipline?: Performance studies at the university of Sydney. In: McKenzie, J., Roms, H., & Wee, C. J. W.-L (eds.) *Contesting performance: Global sites of research.* Basingstoke: Palgrave Macmillan, 37–50.

Sambanis, M. (2014) Bewegtes Lernen – unterrichtliches Vorgehen, Effekte, Ursachen. In: Böttger, H. & Gien, G. (eds.) *The Multilingual Brain – Zum neurodidaktischen Umgang mit Mehrsprachigkeit.* Eichstätt: Academic Press UG, 118–132.

25

Sambanis, M. (2016) Drama activities in the foreign language classroom – considerations from a Didactic-Neuroscientific perspective. In: Even, S. & Schewe, M. (eds.) *Performatives Lehren, Lernen, Forschen. Performative Teaching, Learning, Research.* Berlin: Schibri, 206–221.

Schechner, R. (2003) *Performance theory.* London: Routledge.

Schechner, R. (2013) *Performance studies: An introduction*, 3rd ed. London: Routledge.

Schewe, M. (2013) Taking stock and looking ahead: Drama pedagogy as a gateway to a performative teaching and learning culture. *Scenario* 2(1), 5–23.

Schön, D. (1983) *The reflective practitioner: How professionals think in action.* London: Temple Smith.

Searle, J. R. (1969) *Speech acts: An essay in the philosophy of language.* Cambridge: Cambridge University Press.

Silverberg, L. (1994) *The Sanford Meisner approach: An actor's workbook – workbook one.* New Hampshire: Smith and Kraus.

Tauber, R. T. & Sargent Mester, C. (2007) *Acting lessons for teachers: Using performance skills in the classroom*, 2nd ed. Westport CT: Praeger.

Chapter 2

Mirror, mirror... reflecting on and reviewing your teaching performance

> "Academics seem to be locked up in their minds, always judging, critiquing, and evaluating. That's part of the job. But to be a great teacher you have to let that go, turn it off, and just move like water with the flow. Save the self-reflection and critique for after the last student leaves the room."
>
> **Megan Bylsma, Interview 8**

Before we delve into aspects of performance as a teacher, we need to reflect on and review how we teach currently. In Chapter 1, we identified some of the potential anxieties that might be experienced by (new) teachers in higher education. These anxieties may manifest themselves in different ways in different people, sometimes in very obvious, visible, and conscious manifestations, such as speaking too fast, stuttering, fiddling with an object like a pen or an item of jewellery, or in more extreme cases, in physical shaking or sweating. Or, the teacher may not display obvious signs of any anxieties, but there may still be some impact on performance, and it might only be possible to identify these by reflecting quite deeply on what happens when you teach; how you feel; what you do; how you look; how you are perceived by others; and how you *perform*.

As teachers, we often hear and read about the importance of developing ourselves as reflective practitioners who are able to engage in meaningful reflection on our teaching practice in order to strive for continuous improvements, with the ultimate goal of enhancing the learning experiences of our students. In this chapter, we start by outlining what we mean by reflection before discussing two useful tools to aid reflection and identification of aspects of good practice as well as areas which can be developed further. Here, we focus on lesson observations and microteaching sessions.

REFLECTION AND REFLECTIVE PRACTICE

In order to reflect on, and then attempt to improve our teaching performance, we first need to be clear about what we mean by reflection.
This is both a simple question, you may even think one which has
an obvious and a simple answer, and yet it is also rather complex.
Reflection is simple because it is part of our common vocabulary,
for example in performance reviews in the workplace, where we are
required to reflect on our performance and agree future goals with a
line manager or a supervisor. However, reflection is also a complex
construct, partly because we now live very busy lives, both profes-
sionally and personally, but also because as academics and teachers,
we are used to thinking and writing descriptively and analytically.
Academic writing, and much of the work of an academic, does not
always invite explicit and deep reflection. For this reason, engaging in
reflection on your practice and performance as a teacher can initially
seem challenging.

The American philosopher and educator, John Dewey, emphasised the act of looking back in order to move forward with intention.
In 1910, Dewey started to lay the foundations for what we now term
reflective practice. He considered reflection to be an act which "enables
us to direct our actions with foresight" (Dewey 1910: 6). This means we
consider our practice from a critical perspective, asking questions
about how and why we carried out our work in a given context and
how we can change our practice on the basis of this experience.

The concept of reflective practice was first described explicitly in
1983 by the American philosopher and academic, Donald Schön,
in his seminal work *The Reflective Practitioner: How Professionals
Think in Action*. This book is of particular relevance to us, as Schön's
concept has been applied frequently in teacher education. More
importantly, Schön's views on reflection are pertinent to any practitioner who is considering the performative nature of their work.
Schön described two types of reflection: reflection-on-action and
reflection-in-action, and the latter has implications for our view of
teacher as performer.

Reflection-on-action and reflection-in-action

Schön considers reflection in two distinct contexts. Reflection-on-
action describes a practitioner's thoughts and review of their practice
after the event. As a teacher, reflection-on-action might manifest itself

in a formal discussion with an observer after a class has ended, or you might reflect more informally on your own about how a particular learning activity went, or about why a particular student was not engaged during the class. This is a useful habit and skill to develop, as it encourages you to be a thinking, thoughtful, *reflective* teacher, who is focused on improvement and progress.

Perhaps of particular interest to us is Schön's notion of reflection-in-action. Schön's argument is that technical rationality – the application of science and technical knowledge to solve problems – does not alone account for how we behave in professional practice. For Schön, there is an element of artistry present in the most competent of practitioners. We reflect during the process of working, in the moment, and are able to change our practice on the spot by applying what Schön refers to as knowing-in-action. If something problematic or surprising occurs during a situation, a competent professional is able to respond by drawing on knowledge gained from previous experience. When questioned about this situation, the person may not necessarily provide the correct solution, but is able nevertheless to react favourably in the moment. In short, "competent practitioners usually know more than they can say" (Schön 1983: 8). A useful illustration of Schön's concepts of reflection and knowing-in action is as follows:

Often, a problematic situation presents itself as a unique case [...] A teacher of arithmetic, listening to a child's question, becomes aware of a kind of confusion and, at the same time, a kind of intuitive understanding, for which she has no readily available response. Because the unique case falls outside the categories of existing theory and technique, the practitioner cannot treat it as an instrumental problem to be solved by applying one of the rules in her store of professional knowledge. The case is 'not in the book'. If she is to deal with it competently, she must do so by a kind of improvisation, inventing and testing in the situation strategies of her own devising.

(Schön 1987: 5)

Schön's concept of reflection-in-action is particularly relevant in the context of teaching, especially when considering *performance*. A keyword in the quote from Schön is *improvisation*. By engaging in meaningful reflection, and by developing the ability to reflect-in-action, and therefore improvise, a teacher's performance can be enhanced by reducing anxiety about dealing with unexpected situations in the classroom. The ability to improvise is vital for any performer, and I would argue for any teacher, too. We return to the concept of improvisation in Chapter 6.

Gibbs' reflective Cycle

When beginning the process of reflection, it can be helpful to use a framework or a model to help guide your thinking and reflections. There are many such models, so it is important to find one which you personally find helpful. However, one model which might be useful for our purposes is Gibbs' Reflective Cycle, as it encourages reflection on feelings and emotions. Graham Gibbs published his model in his 1988 book *Learning by Doing*. His work is influenced by David Kolb's experiential learning cycle (Kolb 1984), which proposes that learning takes place through a process of experience, reflection, meaning making, and active experimentation with new strategies.

Gibbs expanded on Kolb's ideas to construct a cycle for debriefing after the event – in a form of reflection-on-action. The cycle incorporates the thoughts and feelings of the person engaged in reflection and consists of six stages. The person engaged in reflection is encouraged to ask questions about themselves and the situation. You can ask yourself questions at each stage to create some distance between yourself and the situation:

1   **Description:** What happened? Where and when did it happen? Who else was present? What did you do? What did others do? What were the outcomes of your and others' actions?

2   **Feeling:** What were you thinking or feeling before the situation? What were you thinking or feeling during the situation? How do you think others felt? How do you feel now?

3   **Evaluation:** What was positive and negative about the experience? What went well? What did not go so well?

4   **Analysis:** What sense can you make of the situation? Why do you think things went well/not so well?

5   **Conclusion:** What else could you have done in this situation? How could it have been a more positive experience? Can you think of any skills that you need to develop to help you deal with the situation more successfully in the future?

6   **Action plan:** If the situation arose again, what would you do? Can you think of one or two concrete actions? What is the timeframe for completion of these actions?

PAUSE FOR REFLECTION:

Think about a time when you have experienced something 'going wrong' during a teaching scenario. Maybe an activity didn't go as well as you had hoped; maybe a student asked a question and you were unable to respond; maybe you felt nervous about an aspect of your teaching and your nerves became visible in class.

Spend a few minutes reflecting on this experience. Work through the stages and prompt questions in Gibbs' reflective cycle.

As mentioned earlier, Gibb's cycle is just one of many models of reflection. It is important to find a framework which works for you; one which enables you to learn from your experiences so that you can begin to reflect, and act, in the moment; in action. We will now look at two tools to aid this reflection on your teaching performance, the first of which is observation.

OBSERVATIONS

When we think of teaching observations, this often conjures up thoughts of quality assurance, which involves checking and monitoring the quality of teaching, whatever we mean by *quality*. This is in part due to the neoliberal agenda in higher education in many countries today. Ball (2012: 29) defines neo-liberalism as "the transformation of social relations into calculabilities and exchanges, that is into the market form, and thus the commodification of educational practice – e.g. in economies of student worth, through performance-related pay, performance management [...]." This brings us back to the point at the beginning of Chapter 1, where we mentioned briefly the dual, opposing views of performance in an increasingly competitive, market-focused higher education system.

Teaching observations in an environment focused on teaching quality, attempting to quantify 'excellence', often have the purpose of managing, checking, rewarding good performance, or identifying poor performance. For our purposes, we are not concerned with this view of performance, which is about management and quantification. We are interested in a much more holistic view of the teacher's performance. Here, we are not talking about observations as a performance management tool, but instead we are using this as a way of sharing and discussing our practice and identifying potential aspects of our teaching performance which can be developed further.

Observations therefore have an important developmental and form-ative purpose and can, and should, be used completely separately from any type of observations which are carried out for performance man-agement purposes. Observations, until relatively recently, were not commonplace in higher education contexts, which is in stark contrast to primary and secondary teaching, where observations are routine (Hatzipanagos & Lygo-Baker 2006). Even observations which are con-ducted with the aim of giving the teacher feedback on their teaching, usually focus on how teaching can be improved in order to enhance students' learning. However, for our purposes in this book, I invite you to be indulgent; to focus purely on yourself, your body, your voice, your skills of presentation, your performance. Of course, in a real teaching scenario, you cannot completely ignore the fact that you also need to ensure that your students have opportunities to learn. The point here is that, when being observed, you need to be clear about the purpose of the observation. If you are initiating an observation to focus on your performativity, you need to make this clear to the observer so that she/he knows what should be the focus of the feedback.

Defining the parameters of the observation

So once you have decided to use observation as a means of gathering initial feedback on your teaching, you can then decide who might be a useful person to act as the observer. This could be any colleague, peer, possibly a student, whose opinions you value and who you think will be able to provide honest, constructive feedback. Most importantly, you need to define why you would like to be observed. As you are the one initiating the observation, it should already be clear that the pur-pose is developmental, and that you are not asking to be observed for performance management purposes. For this reason, it might also be more beneficial to avoid choosing an observer who is used to observ-ing you in a performance management role, such as a line manager or a senior colleague. A peer, who has no link to teaching evaluation or quality assurance, might be a more suitable choice for this type of observation.

Regardless of who acts as the observer, it is important to clarify that the aim of the observation is not only to gain formative feedback, but that you would like the focus to be on *you* – as a teacher – and on your *performance* as a teacher. Otherwise, it is likely that the observer will start to comment on your teaching methods, your interactions with students, to what extent students were learning during the session, and so on. These are obviously all valid and useful, but as I said above, you can be more indulgent in this observation; you can ask the observer to focus less on student learning and more on you and your performance. To many people, this might still sound rather vague, especially to those who are not thinking about the links between teaching and performance. So you can clarify the purpose of the observation even further and ask for feedback on very specific aspects, such as:

- Presentation skills
- Voice projection
- Speech rate
- Intonation
- Use of pauses and silence
- Storytelling
- Use of the teaching space
- Body language
- Eye contact

By speaking in these terms, you make it clear to the observer that you are not asking them to comment on conventional aspects of teaching and learning, but instead on you as an individual teacher; how you present yourself to your 'audience'; how you use your voice and your body to interact with and engage your students.

The focus of the observation may also influence who you choose as an observer. In your local context, you may know people who are particularly good presenters, or who are skilled orators, or who have a particularly strong voice. You can therefore choose your observer according to their skills and expertise. Having said this, everyone has a voice and a body, and each individual observer is able to offer different insights and perspectives. From an observation, you gain one person's view of your teaching performance. To make this a more useful exercise, you could identify several observers in order to gather feedback from multiple perspectives.

The final point to consider when defining the parameters of the observation is the location and the type of teaching you would like to receive feedback on. If you have asked your observer to focus on voice projection, for example, you might choose to be observed in a large teaching space, such as a lecture theatre. If you are interested in gaining feedback on your body language and eye contact, and how you interact with students, perhaps a smaller, more interactive session would be more fruitful.

So observations are one tool that can be used to gather initial feedback on your teaching performance. As we have discussed, the purpose of the observation needs to be clarified, and there needs to be a clear distinction between performance management and developmental feedback to improve performance. Observations clearly rely on the opinions and perspectives of third parties. These can be of great use in helping us to reflect on our teaching and how we perform in the teacher role. However, as suggested in the title of this chapter, it can also be very powerful to hold a mirror up to ourselves when we are teaching so that we can see for ourselves how we look, how we present ourselves as teachers, and start to reflect on the extent to which our internal feelings and emotions match what we see when we observe ourselves. One way of observing yourself is through microteaching.

MICROTEACHING

Another useful tool to facilitate reflection on teaching practice is microteaching, a technique which was developed at the School of Education at Stanford University in 1963 (Allen 1967). Microteaching was originally conceived for the training of pre-service teachers, but it is now also used in many universities as part of pedagogic training of new lecturers. The original concept of microteaching is summarised as follows:

> Microteaching is a scaled down teaching encounter. In microteaching, however, the complexities of the normal teaching encounter have been reduced and the level of feedback to the teacher has been greatly increased [...] From a purely descriptive point of view, microteaching is quite simple. Its basic elements are a teacher, the microclass (usually four or five pupils), a short lesson of five to twenty minutes, and predetermined objectives which have been stated for the particular microteaching occasion.
>
> (Allen & Eve 1968: 181)

So in essence, microteaching is a teaching encounter in a controlled, 'safe' environment. The teacher might engage with this technique for a variety of reasons, including training, identification of good practice and areas for development, or as a space to try out new, innovative approaches. A key feature of microteaching, as explained in the quote above, is the simplification of the teaching encounter, where the complexities of teaching are reduced. This brings us back to our discussion in Chapter 1 of teaching as an artistic endeavour. We drew on the emeritus professor of education, Mike Fleming, who explains that "[a]rt simplifies in order to explore complexity" (Fleming 2016: 200). A parallel can be drawn here to microteaching, where the teaching encounter is simplified, enabling the teacher and the observers to focus on one defined aspect of the teacher's performance, which facilitates a more complex discussion about the particular aspect under scrutiny in the microteaching scenario.

Principles of microteaching

According to the original concept of microteaching, there are five principles, or 'conditions' that need to be present (Allen & Eve 1968: 181):

1   Microteaching involves real teaching, though it is acknowledged by the teacher and students that the purpose of coming together is for practice and development.
2   The complexities of teaching are reduced, such as the number of students, the length of the lesson, and so on.
3   The focus of the teacher's practice is narrowed so that feedback can be gathered on one particular aspect of the teacher's performance, such as interactions with students, use of the voice, assessment methods, and so on.
4   A high degree of structure and control is embedded in the session.
5   The amount of feedback received by the teacher is greatly increased through immediate evaluation of the session using the teacher's own reflections, the students' reactions, comments from tutors facilitating the microteaching session, and watching parts of the session back on video.

An early version of microteaching used at Stanford University followed a five-stage procedure:

1   5-minute microteaching session
2   10-minute critique and feedback
3   15-minute break for the teacher to plan changes to the session
4   5-minute 'reteach' to a different group of students
5   10-minute critique and feedback

In early studies of student ratings of teachers' performances following this microteaching procedure, there was initially no statistically significant improvement from first lesson teach to first lesson reteach. However, significant improvements were found between first lesson teach and second lesson reteach (Allen 1967). This seemed to show that microteaching, as a developmental tool, was best used in the longer term rather than as a one-off diagnostic technique.

In many microteaching sessions used in higher education, the conditions outlined above are largely adhered to, though it is not necessarily the case that teachers attend microteaching sessions multiple times, that is, they do not necessarily engage in reteach sessions. Some changes might be made to suit the local context and the needs of the individual teacher. For example, it is common not to use 'real' students but instead to teach a microteaching session to a small group of colleagues or peers (see Figure 2.1), particularly in situations where academic colleagues are enrolled on a pedagogic training course, such as a Postgraduate Certificate of Education, for example.

Most useful for our purposes in this book are two elements in particular: the controlled, simplified teaching context and the use of

FIGURE 2.1 Photographic still of a Microteaching session

video recording. The precise set up of the microteaching session may vary; more important is the focus of the session, that is, what aspect of teaching does the teacher want to practise – without having to consider all other factors? In contrast to observations, where feedback and perspectives come from third parties, the video recording in microteaching enables the teacher to actually *see* and analyse her or his own performance. As Miltz (1978: 103) puts it: "Videotape media [...] act as the mirror."

Benefits and limitations of microteaching

Microteaching has now been in use for over 50 years, though it has only become prevalent in higher education more recently. During this time, many studies have been conducted to ascertain the benefits and limitations of this technique. In Canada, for example, Troop et al. (2015) investigated the effects of microteaching on Graduate Teaching Assistants' self-efficacy as teachers – the belief that they can perform the role of teacher successfully. They found an increase in self-efficacy for all participants in the study. Numerous other studies, in a variety of types of educational institution, and in various countries, have found evidence of several recurring benefits and limitations. Table 2.1 shows some of these benefits and limitations, as derived from the literature in a study by Ralph (2014).

> But we also have to be aware that actors are trained to act in front of a camera, because it's not natural to just 'continue as normal' with a camera pointing at you. So there is a question about whether a teacher will be 'performing' authentically as soon as a camera is there.
>
> Anna McNamara, Interview 9

The key benefit of microteaching for our purpose, focusing on performativity, is the use of video recording. For many people, the idea of watching themselves on video is uncomfortable, as we gain a rare, objective view of ourselves. However, microteaching participants frequently name analysis of video footage as one of the main benefits of microteaching. The microteaching technique explained above is a formalised, structured session; however, this does not have to be the case. Performing artists often film themselves and their peers informally, using their mobile phones and tablets. For example, research with dance students shows how immediate, informal self and peer

TABLE 2.1 Benefits and limitations of microteaching (adapted from Ralph 2014: 20)

Benefits	Limitations
Positive results from numerous studies of microteaching	Requires multiple sessions to gain significant benefits
Provides opportunities for experiential learning and a focus on practice	Learning may not be transferred to the real teaching context
Breaks teaching down into separate skills	Reduces teaching to discrete skills; potentially loses the bigger picture
Provides a controlled environment and enables the teacher to focus on one aspect of practice	Lacks reality and authenticity
Promotes reflection on practice	All participants must be engaged and willing to provide feedback
Helps to increase confidence and allay anxieties about teaching	Teaching peers may be stressful; fear of losing face
Provides an abundance of feedback from multiple sources – peers, tutors, self, video	
The opportunity to review performance on video is a significant benefit	
All participants learn from each other – including those participating in the student role	
Provides a space to try out new, innovative approaches in a low-stakes environment	

review of video footage can help dancers to make connections between how they felt during the dance and how they looked on camera, helping to address differences between self-perception and perception by onlookers (Buday & Jones 2015). As teachers, we can apply this technique to our own practice, provided we have permission from students to film segments of the lesson. This is clearly different from microteaching as a controlled teaching opportunity, but it is an alternative in which video footage acts as the mirror, enabling us to reflect on our performance.

Reflection is an essential part of teaching, and an important means to help us to develop our practice. As we gain more experience, we can start to reflect and adapt in the moment, using Donald Schön's notion of reflection-in-action. However, to return to the quote from Megan Bylsma at the beginning of this chapter, it is also important not to allow reflective thoughts to hinder our performance in the moment. In the long term, a balance of reflection-in-action and reflection-on-action is likely to aid the development of our teaching performance.

PAUSE FOR REFLECTION:

Do you already have in mind aspects of your teaching performance that you would like to improve? Consider how the tools discussed in this chapter might help you to begin reflecting on your practice so that you can identify which performative aspects to develop further.

 REFERENCES AND FURTHER READING

Allen, D. W. (1967) *Microteaching, a description.* Stanford Teacher Education Program. Available at: https://files.eric.ed.gov/fulltext/ED019224.pdf (accessed 17.10.19).

Allen, D. W. & Eve, A. W. (1968) Microteaching. *Theory into Practice* 7(5), 181–185.

Ball, S. J. (2012) *Global Education Inc. New Policy Networks and the Neo-Liberal Imaginary.* London: Routledge.

Buday, C. & Jones, E. (2015) Self and peer review in dance classes using personal video feedback. In: C. Stock & P. Germanin-Thomas (eds) *Contemporising the past: envisaging the future. Proceedings of the 2014 World Dance Alliance Global Summit.* Available at: https://ausdance.org.au/publications/details/contemporising-the-past-envisaging-the-future (accessed 17.10.19).

Dewey, J. (1910) *How we think.* Boston: D. C. Heath.

Fleming, M. (2016) Exploring the concept of performative teaching and learning. In: S. Even, & M. Schewe, (eds.) *Performatives Lehren, Lernen, Forschen. Performative Teaching, Learning, Research.* Berlin: Schibri, 189–205.

Gibbs, G. (1988) *Learning by doing: A guide to teaching and learning methods.* Oxford: Oxford Centre for Staff and Learning Development.

Hatzipanagos, S. & Lygo-Baker, S. (2006) Teaching observations: A meeting of minds? *International Journal of Teaching and Learning in Higher Education* 17(2), 97–105.

Kolb, D. A. (1984) *Experiential learning: Experience as the source of learning and development.* Englewood Cliffs: Prentice Hall.

Miltz, R. J. (1978) Application of microteaching for teaching improvement in higher education. *British Journal of Teacher Education* 4(2), 103–112.

Ralph, E. G. (2014) The effectiveness of microteaching: Five years' findings. *International Journal of Humanities, Social Sciences and Education* 1(7), 17–28.

Schön, D. A. (1983) *The reflective practitioner: How professionals think in action.* London: Temple Smith.

Schön, D. A. (1987) *Educating the reflective practitioner: Toward a new design for teaching and learning in the professions.* San Francisco: Jossey-Bass.

Troop, M., Wallar, L. & Aspenlieder, E. (2015) Developing graduate students' self-efficacy with learner-centred lecturing. *Canadian Journal of Higher Education* 45(3), 15–33.

Chapter 3

Performance anxiety and stage fright

> "When I feel the butterflies, I direct the energy into a wider and wider smile back stage. If there is a mirror, look at yourself smiling this energy. Now you're ready to perform for others."
>
> **Kate Nasser, Interview 3**

As we have seen in Chapter 1, there are several characteristics of performance which are also present when we are teaching. Notably, there is an 'audience' – students who are hopefully engaged rather than sitting and listening passively to the teacher – and there is an element of self-awareness and reflection on the part of the teacher. The combination of 'performing' in front of others and the teacher's self-awareness can lead to feelings of vulnerability and anxiety. In this chapter, we explore how performers manage their performance anxieties and stage fright, and suggest some techniques to help reduce anxiety and improve performance in the teaching context.

WHAT IS PERFORMANCE ANXIETY?

If you have ever had to perform in front of an audience, whether on stage, at work, at a family gathering, in sport, or in an assessment, it is likely that you have experienced some degree of performance anxiety. Maybe you have performed in the traditional sense, like an actor, a singer, or a musician performing on stage; or maybe you have given a presentation at work or at a conference; or perhaps you have given a speech or a reading at a family occasion. Of course, in the context of this book, maybe you are now considering teaching as a performance. In each of these scenarios, though they are all very different, the common denominator is the presence of an audience and the 'performer's' self-awareness.

PAUSE FOR REFLECTION:

Think about your everyday life; your life at home, with family and friends; your life at work; your social life. Can you identify the scenarios in which you 'perform'? Think about situations where you feel nervous or anxious; situations where you experience 'performance anxiety'. By identifying your performance spaces and the scenarios which have the potential to cause anxiety, you are taking the first step to addressing this issue.

The terms 'performance anxiety' and 'stage fright' are often used interchangeably to refer to psychological and physical responses caused when a person is required to perform in front of an audience. This audience may be real and present or merely anticipated and remote, for example, performing in front of a camera. It is difficult to quantify how many people experience performance anxiety, but several surveys provide evidence that around 75% of people experience some degree of anxiety about public performance (e.g. Hamilton 2014). What is more, we know that those who might be deemed professional performers, such as actors, singers, etc., are not immune to performance anxiety. This tells us that performance anxiety is not caused by a lack of performance *experience*, and to some extent, a certain amount of anxiety might be positive, or even desirable. In reference to music performance anxiety (MPA) specifically, psychoanalyst and concert pianist, Julie Nagel, says:

> Performance anxiety can be mystifying. While it comes alive on stage, performance anxiety does not begin on stage, nor is it the private domain of musicians. Stage fright is ubiquitous. [...] Performance anxiety can be better understood, and, with understanding, this diabolical threat can become facilitating rather than debilitating.
>
> (Nagel 2017: 2–3)

As Nagel highlights, performance anxiety does not appear completely without warning. This is important because it means we can take steps to prepare for the anxieties we might experience, and therefore start to reduce the potentially negative effects on our performance. We can also start to recognise that it does not have to be debilitating. This idea that performance anxiety can be positive is not new. The psychologists, Robert M. Yerkes and John Dillingham Dodson developed the Yerkes Dodson Law in 1908. Their model, sometimes referred to as the Arc of Anxiety (Yerkes & Dodson 1908), illustrates how a certain amount of anxiety can have a positive impact on performance.

> The other thing we know too is that we usually give our best performances in the context of anxiety. So thinking about stage fright as something that we need to completely get rid of is not a very adaptive way to think about it. We actually do worse if we have zero anxiety. So you can actually think of it as a point of power instead of a point of weakness.
>
> Lindsay Masland, Interview 2

The arc in Yerkes Dodson Law shows how performance is enhanced by a certain amount of anxiety – or arousal in Yerkes and Dodson's (1908) original terms (see Figure 3.1). With a low level of anxiety, the person may experience a lack of motivation or even sleepiness. As arousal increases, the person becomes more alert, until an optimal level of arousal is reached at the top of the arc. At this point, the anxiety experienced by the person impacts positively on the performance. As levels of anxiety increase beyond the optimum, the person starts to experience negative effects. At this point, the person becomes stressed and the level of the performance is impacted, shown by the falling arc in the Yerkes-Dodson curve.

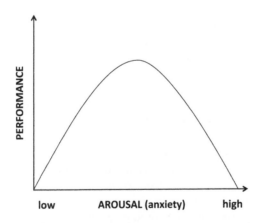

FIGURE 3.1 Adapted, simplified version of the Yerkes-Dodson curve

The Arc of Anxiety provides us with a simple visual representation of the relationship between anxiety (arousal) and performance. It tells us that we should not aim to eradicate anxiety completely when we are in a state of performance; we need a certain amount of anxiety in order to become energised and to perform at our best. It follows, therefore, that we need to be aware of the symptoms of performance anxiety so that we can recognise them and begin to understand our own optimal level of anxiety.

A NOTE ON TEACHING ANXIETY

In Chapter 1, I identified some of the common anxieties experienced by new teachers, mainly from my own conversations and interactions with colleagues (see Table 1.1). However, teaching anxiety is not only experienced by those who are relatively new to university teaching. Fraser et al. (2007) point out that even experienced teachers report anxieties about various aspects of their teaching performance. The same can be said of anyone in a performance role: even experienced actors, singers, and public speakers report experiencing performance anxiety and stage fright. Research on teaching anxiety has been conducted for several decades (e.g. Bernstein 1983; Keavney & Sinclair 1978), which in itself demonstrates the extent and importance of this phenomenon.

Numerous studies have identified a variety of sources of teaching anxiety, such as heavy workload (Borg 1990) and job insecurity (Tytherleigh et al. 2005). In addition, Gardner and Leak (1994) identified three categories of teaching anxiety related to performance: preparation for teaching, anticipation of teaching, and interaction in the classroom. These categories map well onto the common anxieties identified in Table 1.1. Specifically in the context of lecturing, Exley and Dennick (2009) outline commonly cited sources of teaching anxiety, all of which are about performance:

- Lack of confidence – what if students in the 'audience' know more about the topic than I do?
- Alien experience – it is not an everyday experience for a teacher to stand in a large theatre speaking in front of a large audience.
- Vulnerability – being the centre of attention and feelings that others are judging your 'performance'.
- Self-consciousness – insecurities about voice, image, accent, etc.
- Making mistakes – desire to give a polished performance and avoiding saying the 'wrong thing'.

From the categories above, and from research on teaching anxiety over the years, it is clear that teachers experience performance anxiety. Wong and Chiu (2019) have also found evidence that university teachers place great value on student and teacher enjoyment in learning and that, to some extent, lecturers and tutors fulfil an *entertainment* role. This is all further evidence of the performative nature of teaching.

SYMPTOMS OF PERFORMANCE ANXIETY

Performance anxiety manifests itself in a variety of ways. The symptoms themselves are not anxiety; the symptoms are the manifestation, often visible, of the person's anxiety. There are typically three categories of symptoms: psychological, physical, and cognitive. Psychological symptoms are the emotions and feelings that surface when experiencing performance anxiety. Physical symptoms present themselves in the body and are often visible to the audience. Cognitive symptoms refer to the thoughts and inner narratives that play out in our minds while experiencing performance anxiety (see Table 3.1).

The symptoms in Table 3.1 are adapted from the music performance context (Nagel 2017: 20). Nagel points out that the different categories of symptoms might be experienced alone or in concert, as the mind (psychological and cognitive symptoms) and the body

TABLE 3.1 Example symptoms of performance anxiety

Psychological	Physical	Cognitive
I feel self-conscious.	I am sweating.	I know my students don't like me.
I am worried I will forget answers to key questions.	My hands are shaking.	I will get bad teacher evaluations.
I fear being humiliated.	My heart is beating quickly.	My colleagues will hear about how bad I am at teaching.
I fear looking incompetent.	My breathing is shallow.	I am the worst teacher/ academic ever.
I worry about how my students will respond to me.	My mouth is dry.	I don't want to teach any more.

(physical symptoms) work together. It is apparent from each symptom that there is a clear focus on oneself – on *me* and *I* – and this exacerbates the anxiety, as any perceived negative outcome of the experience is directly linked to the individual personally.

PAUSE FOR REFLECTION:

Think about a time when you have experienced performance anxiety – in a teaching context or otherwise. Do you recognise any of the symptoms in Table 3.1? Have you experienced any symptoms that are not listed? Make a list of the symptoms you have experienced and categorise them as psychological, physical, and cognitive symptoms.

BREATHING AND RELAXATION

An important factor to consider in relation to performance anxiety is breathing. This is something we are all seemingly experts in, as we do it over 17,000 times a day. However, when we become nervous, we start to take shorter breaths, and these shallow breaths in turn exacerbate feelings of anxiety. We live such busy lives and we rarely take time to become consciously aware of our breathing.

> In terms of how I manage it [anxiety], I go back to what I would do as a performer, so preparation, breathing, use your pre-show or pre-teaching rituals, whatever they might be, so perhaps warm-ups, going over my script or notes, making sure I'm aware of the performance space or classroom, doing a tech rehearsal and making sure everything is working. And then being mindful within the performance or during teaching of how nerves can impact upon delivery.
>
> Clare Chandler, Interview 10

QUICK BREATH CHECK:

Do you know how many breaths you take per minute when you are at rest? Take a moment to check this. Sit comfortably, relax, and focus on taking regular breaths. Take a stopwatch and count your breaths over one minute. How many times do you breathe in a minute?

At rest, adults breathe around 12–20 times per minute. This can increase to 40–60 times per minute during physical exercise – or when we are anxious. Performers, especially singers, are highly aware of how their breathing helps or hinders performance. One of the first techniques learned by singers is to breathe diaphragmatically. This is probably something you have heard before, but what does it mean? The diaphragm is the large horizontal muscle beneath the lungs. When we inhale, the diaphragm contracts and lowers. In turn, the volume of the lungs expands and the space is filled with air. When we exhale, the diaphragm relaxes and rises as the air is released. However, we often breathe in a shallow way, from our chest. We will now look at some breathing and relaxation exercises to encourage diaphragmatic, conscious, relaxed breathing.

BREATHING AND RELAXATION EXERCISES

Diaphragmatic breathing

Try this simple exercise to practise diaphragmatic breathing.

1   Lie on your back on a flat surface or in bed, with your knees bent and your head supported.
2   Place one hand on your upper chest and the other just below your rib cage. This will allow you to feel your diaphragm move as you breathe.
3   Breathe in slowly through your nose so that your stomach moves out against your hand. The hand on your chest should remain as still as possible.
4   Tighten your stomach muscles, letting them fall inward as you exhale through pursed lips. The hand on your upper chest should remain as still as possible.

If the hand on your chest is moving, you are breathing from your chest. This leads to shallow breathing. When you breathe in this way, you are breathing more frequently, which is likely to exacerbate feelings of anxiety. By practising this exercise, you will learn to breathe deeply, avoiding shallow breathing. You will also develop a conscious awareness of how you breathe so that you can recognise when your breathing technique is working against you, that is, when your breathing is increasing your performance anxiety.

Box breathing

Another breathing technique used by a variety of people, from performers to athletes to armed forces personnel, is box breathing or four-square breathing. It is recognised as a helpful technique to reduce anxiety and heighten performance and focus. There is evidence that breathing in a controlled and considered way can help to calm the autonomic nervous system, which regulates bodily functions that work without our conscious thought, such as heart rate, breathing, and digestion.

1   Sit upright and slowly exhale through your mouth to empty your lungs.
2   Inhale for 4 seconds.
3   Hold for 4 seconds.
4   Exhale for 4 seconds.
5   Hold for 4 seconds.
6   Repeat several times.

You could also experiment with different lengths of time for the inhalation, hold and exhalation. For example:

1   Inhale for 4 seconds.
2   Hold for 2 seconds.
3   Exhale for 6 seconds.
4   Hold for 2 seconds.

Progressive muscle relaxation

The other aspect here, which is closely linked to breathing, is relaxation. There are many relaxation techniques used by performers and by people in everyday life. One particularly prevalent technique, progressive muscle relaxation, was developed by Dr Edmund Jacobson in 1929. This technique involves contracting and relaxing different muscle groups one at a time and becoming consciously aware of how the body feels after each muscle contraction. Much like the breathing techniques above, this exercise helps to connect mind with body (and muscles).

1   Breathe slowly and regularly through your nose.
2   Tighten each muscle group as you breathe in for 5 seconds. Take care not to strain excessively; tighten the muscles lightly.
3   Release muscles as you breathe out and take 10 seconds to notice any differences in how the muscles feel.

4   Work through the muscles in your body from toes, legs, lower back, chest and abdomen, hands, arms, shoulders, neck, and face.

5   Become aware of how the muscles feel in your whole body and identify any areas where tension remains.

6   Repeat the process of combining breathing with tensing of muscles for the areas where tension remains.

Guided breathing and relaxation

This final exercise is taken from the context of music performance. It can be done by recording a script yourself, working through the steps below. An example of a script to guide you through this exercise can be found in Buswell (2006: 68–73).

1   Lie down with your eyes closed, arms by your side and palms facing up.

2   Let any noises and the ambience of the room float away like clouds.

3   Breathe in for 4 seconds; hold for 2 seconds; breathe out for 6 seconds; pause for 2 seconds. Repeat three times.

4   Continue to breathe normally becoming aware of your stomach rising and falling. If your chest is rising and falling, breathe deeper into your diaphragm.

5   Feel your body sink into the floor as you start to feel heavier.

6   Imagine a warmth spreading from your forehead, over your eyes, into your ears, nose, cheeks, and mouth.

7   Keep your mouth closed; allow your jaw to sag and to become relaxed. Feel the warmth flow down the back of your skull and into your neck and shoulders.

8   Continue breathing, remaining aware of your stomach rising and falling, and feel the warmth flow into your arms, elbows, wrists, hands, and fingers.

9   Continue visualising and feeling this warmth work through your body until you reach your toes.

10 Focus again on your breathing, ensuring you are breathing deeply through your nose and that you are breathing into your stomach, not your chest.

11 When you are ready, maintain your regular breathing and count to 10 slowly. When you reach 10, open your eyes and take a moment to notice how your breathing feels.

UNHELPFUL NARRATIVES

One of the most common symptoms (and causes) of performance anxiety is the perpetuation of unhelpful narratives. As we have seen in Table 3.1, we can often help anxieties to increase by building unhelpful stories around negative thoughts. For example: "I am the worst teacher ever" is the initial thought which leads to a whole narrative that perpetuates the original, irrational thought – irrational because it is very unlikely that this person is actually the worst teacher ever.

> So in terms of practical tips: one thing I think – and I tell people who I train – is to just do it! Things are never as bad as you think. Specifically in the teaching context, it's important to make that personal connection with your students; greet them personally at the door. It completely changes the dynamic in the room. Eventually, everyone finds their own way to deal with nerves. They don't go away completely, and they shouldn't go away completely. If you're still nervous – you have butterflies in your stomach – it shows you still care.
>
> Martin Billingham, Interview 6

Shakespeare's *Hamlet* sums up what psychologists tell us about the power of positive (and negative) thinking: "There is nothing either good or bad, but thinking makes it so" (Hamlet, Act 2, Scene 2). If we have a negative experience and then focus on the negative thoughts, feelings, and emotions evoked from that experience, we will continue to experience a negative emotional response and anxiety when confronted with a similar situation in the future. We have to reframe the experience, and retell the story using a more helpful, more optimistic narrative.

The types of unhelpful narratives and negative thoughts are neatly summarised in a co-authored book about stage fright by actor and musician, Mick Berry, and psychologist Dr Michael R. Edelstein. Berry and Edelstein (2009) explain that performances in and of themselves do not induce anxiety; we indulge in negative thinking which leads to some of the symptoms of performance anxiety outlined above. The types of negative, anxiety-inducing narratives are summarised in Table 3.2.

The thought patterns here are similar to the cognitive symptoms of performance anxiety in Table 3.1. By thinking about what *must* happen in a teaching scenario (or in any performance), there is no flexibility for things to go *wrong* – or not according to plan. This sets an almost

TABLE 3.2 Anxiety-inducing negative thoughts (adapted from Berry & Edelstein 2009)

Category	Example Thoughts and Narratives
must-statements	"I must teach well."
	"My students must like me."
	"I must get good teaching evaluations."
	"I must not look nervous or insecure; otherwise, my students will think I am not good enough."
must-statements combined with *awfulizing*	"I must teach well; it will be awful if I don't."
	"It would be awful if my students didn't like me."
	"It would be a disaster if I got bad teaching evaluations; I might lose my job."
	"It would be embarrassing if my students could see that I'm nervous."
Seeking acceptance	"If my students don't like me, it proves I'm not good enough to teach at a university."
	"If my students don't think I'm a credible academic, I will be a total failure."
Perfectionism	"I must teach as well as possible – even perfectly."
	"Other colleagues are brilliant teachers. I have to teach as well as them."
Self-(be)rating	"I'm the worst teacher and academic in the department."
	"If I continue to get such bad teaching evaluations, my career will never progress."
Anxiety about anxiety	"I must not be nervous."
	"If I'm anxious, my hands will shake and I will start to sweat. My students will notice and it will be embarrassing."

impossible task for the teacher-performer. Once we are in such a negative mindset, it is easy to start engaging in *awfulizing* – in exaggerating the consequences of not fulfilling our self-induced *musts*. This is exacerbated further by making self-worth dependent on an external, largely uncontrollable factor, for example, being liked by your students. The unhelpful narrative continues with self-berating, focusing on perceived negatives about oneself. Finally, performance anxiety is compounded as the person becomes aware of increasing anxiety and becomes anxious about being anxious!

PAUSE FOR REFLECTION:

Do you recognise any of these negative thought patterns? Some of them may appear extreme, but the examples serve to illustrate the point: that we have the power to exacerbate or reduce performance anxiety by changing the inner narratives that we tell ourselves. Can you think of any examples of when you have engaged in unhelpful narratives, in a teaching context or otherwise?

REFRAMING AND RETELLING THE STORY

Many of us have spent many years listening to – and believing – negative inner narratives. A useful way to start reducing performance anxiety is to reframe negative experiences by retelling narratives in a positive light. One technique, developed by the American psychologist and educator, Dr Martin Seligman, is the ABCDE technique (Seligman 2006):

Adversity: objective, 'truth statements' about an event which induced anxiety.

Beliefs: negative thoughts that were running through your head during/about the event.

Consequences: what were you thinking/feeling as a result of these beliefs? How did you react?

Dispute: think of a rebuttal to your irrational beliefs; think of a more optimistic alternative belief.

Energy: how has reframing your beliefs changed your energy and mood? Do you view the experience differently?

We could apply this technique to performance anxiety in teaching. Imagine a university teacher has just taught her first tutorial. Many of the students were rather quiet, and it was difficult to engage them in discussion:

A: I taught my first tutorial last week and it didn't go very well.

B: The students weren't very engaged and the session just felt very flat. They didn't think I was a very good teacher.

C: I became very nervous and started talking very fast, trying to fill the silence when students refused to answer my questions.

I started to sweat and I felt embarrassed. I don't think I'm going to do well as an academic and I don't want to teach any more.

D: But actually, there were at least three students who were very engaged. They asked several good questions and responded with enthusiasm during discussions. Maybe some of the other students, who didn't respond directly to my questions, also learned something from the session.

E: Upon reflection, the tutorial didn't go as badly as I thought. It is easy to focus on perceived negatives. There were some students who were disengaged, but others seemed to enjoy the session. It's not the end of the world if some students didn't enjoy one tutorial, and it is irrational to conclude that I'm not going to be a good academic because of one (perceived) negative experience.

It is very common to focus on perceived negatives when we are teaching. From my own experience, I have often found that it is too easy to focus on the one (or two) students who were not engaged or who did not seem to enjoy the session, easily forgetting that other students gave excellent answers to questions and seemed to enjoy the learning experience. The same is true of course in teaching evaluations. It is easy to focus on one negative evaluation and draw general, negative conclusions about your teaching, ignoring the other, more positive evaluations. Using a technique like ABCDE can raise awareness of negative thought patterns and prompt us to retell the narrative more positively, or at least in a more balanced, rational way.

Another example of reframing, adapted from Berry and Edelstein (2009), is my own narrative and (performance) anxiety about writing this book. As I write the chapters, my thoughts might go – and have gone – as follows:

Story

I think teaching is a performative act and I strongly believe that techniques from the performing arts can help university teachers to increase their confidence and ultimately help them to teach better. I am putting my thoughts and beliefs out in the public domain, and this book *must* be well received. What if people don't agree with my ideas? What if people don't like how I write? I might lose credibility among my peers and colleagues.

These are slightly exaggerated negative thoughts and self-doubts that I have experienced while thinking about and writing this book. These thoughts are irrational and emphasise the 'worst case scenario'. Retelling the story might go as follows:

Re-story

I strongly believe that techniques from the performing arts can help university teachers to increase their confidence and ultimately help them to teach better. There is already evidence that taking a performative view of teaching can be beneficial for teachers and students. However, it doesn't matter if people disagree. It is unlikely that everyone who reads this book will agree with my ideas, or that everyone will like how I write – and this is fine, and normal. Some readers and colleagues will find the book useful, and this is rewarding.

PAUSE FOR REFLECTION:

Think about a time when you have experienced performance anxiety, preferably in a teaching context. Work through the ABCDE technique. Focus particularly on the D and E – dispute your negative narrative and reframe it, noticing how you view the experience in a more positive, balanced, rational light.

VISUALISATION

Reframing negative narratives is one way of ensuring negative thoughts are not given the power to cause performance anxiety. This can be taken a step further by focusing not just on thoughts, but also on the visual representation of an experience. Visualisation is not a new technique; however, the concept gained greater prominence in 1978 following the publication of a book by the American personal development specialist, Shakti Gawain: *Creative Visualisation: Use the Power of Your Imagination to Create What You Want in Life*. The premise behind visualisation is that thoughts are the precursor to action and creation. Shakti Gawain explains it as follows:

Thought is a quick, light, mobile form of energy [...] When we create something, we always create it first in thought form. A thought or idea always precedes manifestation. 'I think I'll make dinner' is the idea that precedes creation of a meal. 'I want a new dress' precedes going and buying a new one [...] Simply having an idea or thought, holding it in your mind, is an energy that will tend to attract and create that form on the material plane.

(Gawain 2016: 10)

The concept of visualisation builds on what we have discussed in relation to unhelpful narratives and re-telling stories in a positive light. Visualisation techniques are used by people in a variety of contexts, from the creative and performing arts to sport, to education and health. It is a way of shifting focus away from anxiety-inducing thoughts and onto the desired outcome.

Visualisation exercise

This basic visualisation technique is adapted from Gawain (2016: 13–16):

1 Sit or lie down in a relaxed position. Starting at your toes, tense and relax each muscle in your body, working up to your head (see progressive muscle relaxation above).
2 Practise deep, slow, diaphragmatic breathing.
3 Count down slowly from 10 to 1, feeling yourself become more relaxed as you get closer to 1.
4 Think of a teaching scenario going exactly as you would like it to go. Picture yourself in the classroom, lecture theatre, or laboratory. Picture those around you. Focus on the sounds, the smells, and the ambience of the room. Focus on how you feel; how confident you feel in the teacher role. Play with these thoughts for a while until you have created a positive, empowering image.
5 Keep the image in your mind and make some positive, affirmative statements about the situation (aloud or in your head), such as "this is an excellent lesson"; "I really enjoy teaching, and my students are learning a lot."
6 Continue the visualisation for as long as you find it enjoyable and empowering. Repeat it as often as you can in order to strengthen the positive thoughts.

THE STANISLAVSKI SYSTEM

At this point, I want to mention briefly the Stanislavski System – a set of techniques developed in the 1900s by the influential Russian actor and theatre director, Konstantin Stanislavski. Visualisation is one part of the Stanislavski System, which still forms the basis of training for many actors and performers today. The System is highly complex and detailed, but its fundamental aim is to help actors create believable characters and emotions by developing a deep empathy for the character. This was highly innovative at the time, when thespians in 19th century Russia adopted flamboyant and grandiose gestures and tones, which did not resemble how people moved and spoke in real life.

As I argued in Chapter 1, teaching is not the same as acting, and not all performances are an *act*. However, there are some aspects of Stanislavski's methods which might be useful when considering teaching performance. Visualisation is one technique in the System, and this might be used to imagine our teaching performance playing out how we would like, and start to change negative narratives about our performance. We will come back to other aspects of the Stanislavski System later, such as motivation and re-education when we discuss the body and lecturing in Chapter 5, and the use of the 'Magic If' when we discuss improvisation in Chapters 6 and inclusive teaching in Chapter 7.

> The biggest thing I have to remember when I get a case of the nerves is the things I learned from improv theatre: laughter signals to the audience you are okay if you mess up and this makes it okay for them to feel okay too.
>
> Megan Bylsma, Interview 8

In this chapter, we have explored how breathing and relaxation techniques can help us to cope with anxieties about teaching and performance. If we become anxious and start to use poor breathing technique, it is likely that our voice will be affected, leading, for example, to a shaky, shrill sound. We take a closer look at the voice in our next chapter.

 ## REFERENCES AND FURTHER READING

Bernstein, D. A. (1983) Dealing with teaching anxiety: A personal view. *Journal of the National Association of Colleges and Teachers of Agriculture* 27, 4–7.

Berry, M. & Edelstein, M. R. (2009) *Stage fright. 40 Stars tell you how they beat America's #1 fear.* Tucson: See Sharp Press.

Borg, M. (1990) Occupational stress in British educational settings: A review. *Educational Psychology* 10(2), 103–127.

Buswell, D. (2006) *Performance strategies for musicians.* Hertfordshire: MX Publishing.

Cavanagh, S. R. (2016) *The spark of learning: Energizing the college classroom with the science of emotion.* Morgantown, WV: West Virginia University Press.

Exley, K. & Dennick, R. (2009) *Giving a lecture. From presenting to teaching,* 2nd ed. Oxford: Routledge.

Fraser, I. H., Houlihan, M., Fenwick, K., Fish, T., & Möller, C. (2007) Teaching anxiety and teaching methods of university professors: A correlational analysis. *American Association of Behavioral and Social Sciences Journal,* 78–90.

Gardner, L. E. & Leak, G. K. (1994) Characteristics and correlates of teaching anxiety among college psychology teachers. *Teaching of Psychology* 21(1), 28–32.

Gawain, S. (2016) *Creative visualisation: Use the power of your imagination to create what you want in your life,* 4th ed. Novato, California: Nataraj Publishing.

Hamilton, C. (2014) *Communicating for Results. A Guide for Business and the Professions.* Boston, MA: Wadsworth.

Jacobson, E. (1929) *Progressive Relaxation.* Oxford: University of Chicago Press.

Keavney, G. & Sinclair, K. E. (1978) Teacher concerns and teacher anxiety: A neglected topic of classroom research. *Review of Educational Research* 48(2), 273–290.

Nagel, J. J. (2017) *Managing stage fright: A guide for musicians and music teachers.* New York: Oxford University Press.

Seligman, M. E. P. (2006) *Learned optimism: How to change your mind and your life,* 2nd ed. New York: Vintage.

Tytherleigh, M. Y., Webb, C., Cooper, C. L., & Ricketts, C. (2005) Occupational stress in UK higher education institutions: A comparative study of all staff categories. *Higher Education Research and Development* 24(1), 41–61.

Wong, B., & Chiu, Y-L. T. (2019) Let me entertain you: The ambivalent role of university lecturers as educators and performers. *Educational Review* 71(2), 218–233.

Yerkes, R. M. & Dodson, J. D. (1908) The relationship of strength of stimulus to rapidity of habit formation. *Journal of Comparative Neurology and Psychology* 18, 459–482.

Chapter 4

The voice

> "Voice tone. It is the simplest mechanism to lend meaning and emphasis to words. Louder, softer, pitch, pace, pauses – all create a story telling ambiance that draws people in."
>
> **Kate Nasser, Interview 3**

The voice is arguably a teacher's most important tool – or instrument. It is also often misused and neglected, resulting in vocal problems, which in turn can have a negative impact on teaching performance. In this chapter, we take a look at the voice to understand how we produce sound. You will be invited to get to know your own voice and experiment with some exercises to help project a more resonant sound. Particularly important is awareness of how you use your voice so that you become used to speaking in ways which limit any potential damage to your voice, and instead, enable your voice to increase the impact of your message. The renowned voice and acting coach, Patsy Rodenburg, explains in *The Right to Speak* that we can all improve how we sound and how we speak; a good voice is not a gift bestowed just upon performers. We can all benefit from understanding better how our voices work, and do regular vocal exercises to keep our voices strong.

> To the layperson what an actor does with their voice seems amazing but they do know how to physically exercise their voice and prepare. This work is not hard when understood but few understand it.
>
> (Rodenburg 2015: 2)

THE VOICE AND VOCAL ANATOMY

It is clear from common experience that our voices are quite unique and vary widely. If a friend or a relative calls you on the phone, you can often easily recognise their voice without hearing their name. However, every person's voice consists of three main components:

- Respiration
- Phonation
- Articulation

Vocal anatomy does not consist of one discrete organ or region of the body: variations, disturbances or damage in one of several areas will affect our perception of a person's voice (Calais-German and German 2016). **Respiration** is the voice's generator, breathing, which we looked at in Chapter 3. We inhale air, which causes the diaphragm to contract and lower, expanding the volume of the lungs. At this stage, we have not produced any voiced sound. If you are breathing heavily, or even moderately, you can hear the inhalation and exhalation of air through your nose and/or mouth, but there is no vibration at this point. This is produced by the second component in your vocal anatomy.

In order to use breath to produce voiced sounds, **phonation**, we need to create vibrations. These vibrations start in the **larynx** – or the voice box. The larynx houses the **vocal folds**, thin muscles which vibrate to create sound. As we breathe normally, air moves between the open vocal folds, and we do not produce sound. When we produce sound, however, we exhale air and the vocal folds are pulled together and begin to vibrate. The faster the vocal folds vibrate, the higher the pitch of the sound produced. If you sing a simple scale, notes at the lower end of the scale are at a lower pitch than notes at the higher end of the scale, and the notes with higher pitch cause the vocal folds to vibrate faster than when producing notes at a lower pitch. For example, if you hum the first C (C4) in Figure 4.1, this would cause the vocal folds to vibrate less frequently than in the higher pitch C5 – the last note in the scale which is one octave higher than C4 (you can easily check these notes using a free online piano – unless you have a real one!). At this point, the sound is heard as a buzz or a hum, but we have not yet created any discernible speech.

FIGURE 4.1 C-major scale

Speech sounds, such as recognisable words and letters of the alphabet, are created by **articulation,** also called resonation. The buzzy vibrations formed by the vocal folds are then turned into speech by muscle contractions in the pharynx – Greek for 'throat' – and by using different areas of the mouth to create different sounds. You can check which parts of the mouth are used to form different sounds. For example, the /θ/ sound as in 'breath' is produced by placing the tongue towards the back of your top front teeth.

QUICK ARTICULATOR CHECK:

Which articulators – which parts of the mouth – do you use to produce these sounds?

/p/ as in '**p**lay'
/f/ as in '**f**ly'
/k/ as in '**k**ite'
/h/ as in '**h**ome'

This is not a book on articulatory phonetics, but it is useful to raise our awareness of how and where different sounds are produced. In the examples above, the /p/ sound is a 'bilabial consonant', produced by restricting the air flow between both top and bottom lips. The /f/ sound is a 'labiodental', created by connecting the top teeth and the bottom lip. The /k/ sound is a 'velar sound', produced by the back of the tongue moving up towards the soft palate (velum). The /h/ sound is a 'voiceless glottal fricative'. When you say /home/, you should notice that there is no vibration on the /h/ sound – it is voiceless. The vibration – voice – starts on the vowel /o/. We return to this later in this chapter when we discuss improving pronunciation and articulation.

A final point to mention in relation to voice – and vocal anatomy – is that we can all improve our voice. With specific reference to singing, Friedlander (2018) explains that vocal performance is a trainable skill;

it is not necessarily an innate gift – or lack thereof. Some people may be born with physical advantages which help them to produce a rich, resonant sound, but practice and improved technique can improve a person's singing voice. This is important for us as teachers, as it means we can all improve our 'vocal performance', regardless of what we believe about our voices. If you tell yourself "I have a horrible voice" or "I can't sing", think again!

FUNDAMENTALS

We return briefly to the importance of breathing. In Chapter 3, we discussed the importance of abdominal or diaphragmatic breathing, rather than breathing in a very shallow way in your chest. However, diaphragmatic breathing can sometimes inadvertently lead to erratic intakes of breath. We erroneously think we have to breathe in as much air as possible, as quickly as possible. You can check your technique by looking in a mirror while you practise diaphragmatic breathing. Is your chest moving outwards? Are your shoulders moving upwards? Are you gasping as you take in a deep breath? If you notice any of these things, this means you are still breathing from your chest. We some- times find ourselves gasping for air because we think we are taking in a 'deep' breath; but in this case, we are simply taking in a lot of air. The aim is not necessarily to breathe in as much air as possible; instead, the aim is to breathe in a supported way – using the diaphragm for support – and to use the inhaled air to carry your sound (voice).

> Learning to support my voice using the breath/diaphragm for sing-
> ing was directly transferable to the classroom as it helped me to pro-
> ject my voice audibly without straining it. That helped me survive a
> period of voice strain, which hasn't recurred since. Studying singing
> also made me more aware of how listening to other people's voices
> can give clues to their underlying emotions and level of confidence,
> which definitely helps with empathy, both as a teacher and trainer.
> David Jay, Interview 4

Exercise: using breath in a more measured way

As you may have seen in the mirror, we are often tempted to inhale a large amount of air in one go and then to exhale all the air in one out-breath. This exercise is sometimes used by singers to train the technique of partially inhaling and exhaling when breath is required, and to help support diaphragmatic breathing.

1   Inhale in 3 repetitions of 3 short sniffs until your lungs are full.
2   Release and allow the air to flow out until you are comfortable. Do not inhale again yet.
3   Now blow out the remaining air in 3 repetitions of 3 short puffs until you have released all the air from your lungs and you feel your abdominal muscles contract.
4   Open your mouth and allow your lungs to fill up again. Be careful not to gasp or breathe in erratically. You should feel your abdominal muscles release and your stomach should move outwards. Your chest should remain still, showing that you are breathing diaphragmatically.

You could try this with a different number of sniffs and puffs, taking care not to over exert yourself. Over time, this technique can be useful for training the abdominal muscles to work in a connected way with your breathing, hence helping to engage your diaphragm. One other exercise, or check, in relation to breathing involves connecting exhalation with breathing. Try the following: take a deep breath and then read the sentence below:

Good morning, today we are going to focus on how we can use our voice more powerfully.

It is quite common for us to take a deep breath, then to release most of the air before speaking. This means we waste a lot of the power and resonance that would have been in the voice if we had used the air to help us speak. If you did this when you read the sentence above, you probably did this without noticing. This is something you can ask observers to look out for when they observe your teaching, and you could self-assess this if you record yourself teaching, either informally or as part of a microteaching session (see Chapter 2). Once you become aware that you are doing this, you can start to breathe-speak-exhale more consciously.

GETTING TO KNOW YOUR VOICE

If you have ever heard a recording of your voice, it is likely that it did not sound as you expected. In fact, many of us cringe at the sound of our own voice. This is such a common phenomenon that there is a name for it: voice confrontation.

> I also have a fairly high natural voice, so I need to be careful – especially when tired or stressed – that it doesn't get screechy. Which means I often use my 'recording' voice – which is still me, just a bit more modulated, slightly more 'sweet' sounding, and a whole lot louder.
>
> Megan Bylsma, Interview 8

QUICK VOICE CHECK:

Take any device with voice recording software. Most mobile phones now have an in-built voice memo function. Record yourself saying a couple of sentences. For example: Hello, my name is Richard and I like the sound of my own voice. You can say anything; it doesn't even have to make sense! Listen back to the recording and notice how it sounds. Does it sound like *you*? Now say the same words again and compare the sound of your voice on the recording to the sound of your voice as you speak the words live. Is there a noticeable difference? Do you like what you hear on the recording?

It is likely that what you hear on the recording is a slightly higher pitch to the voice you usually hear as you are speaking. This is usually explained by the fact that you hear yourself speaking through a combination of sound transferred by air conduction, externally to your ears, and sound transferred internally through vibrations in your bones while you are speaking. These bone vibrations produce lower frequencies, which in turn means you hear a richer, more bass-like voice in your own head. When you listen to a recording of yourself, you are listening only to the external sound, without any of the bone-conducted sound, and you therefore hear your voice how others hear it, which is probably slightly higher pitched than you are used to. This is voice confrontation, where you are confronted with hearing *yourself*, but this *self* does not necessarily correspond to how you hear your voice in your head.

Having said this, the reason we tend to 'dislike' the sound of our own voice might not be explained simply by a mismatch between internal and external frequencies and our expectations about how our voices sound. There is some evidence to show that, when people do not know that a recorded voice is their own, they may engage in vocal implicit

63

egotism – favouring one's own voice over others'. This was found in a study by Hughes and Harrison (2013), where participants rated their own voices significantly more favourably when they were unaware that they were listening to their own voice. It seems, then, that we often dislike hearing our own voice partly because it does not correspond to our expectations, but also because we are hearing ourselves clearly, which can make us feel vulnerable and exposed. In some ways, this is similar to the feelings we might have when we see ourselves on video. You will know how this feels if you have been video recorded while teaching (see Chapter 2). For our purposes, it is not important to have a definitive reason for why voice confrontation occurs. However, as teachers, it is useful to become comfortable with hearing our own voice, so getting to know your voice – its tone, its volume, its colour, its range, its limits – is an important step when considering teaching as a performative act. In addition to this, if you have an awareness of your own voice, you are in a better position to help students develop their voices when contributing during in-class activities or when giving presentations to their peers.

Finding your vocal range

A useful starting point when getting to know your voice is to become familiar with your vocal range. This is something that singers do in order to work out the limits of their range and to find out whether they are a soprano, a tenor, a bass, and so on. Try the following:

1   Using a piano (you can use a free online piano), find Middle C (this should be marked C4 on the key of an online piano).
2   Say a word or a sound to match the note, such as *laa*. Travel down the white keys, saying *laa* (or your chosen word) on each note until you reach the note you can say/sing comfortably.
3   Return to Middle C (C4) and travel up the white keys, singing/ saying each note as you go. Continue until you reach the highest note you can say/sing comfortably.
4   This will give you your comfortable vocal range.

Clearly, we are not particularly concerned with how high or low you can sing. However, it is useful to remind ourselves that we all have a somewhat more extensive vocal range than we realise. When you are speaking in your everyday life, you do not use the full range that you have just identified. However, if you are more aware of how high or low the pitch of your voice *could* go, this will help you to speak in a more varied, interesting way, avoiding a very monotonous tone.

Once you have really listened to your voice – confronted it – and then understood the range of and limits to your voice, you can start to isolate different aspects of your voice which have an impact on performance, namely:

- Tempo
- Rhythm
- Articulation
- Pronunciation
- Pitch
- Volume
- Quality
- Word choice
- Vocal nonverbals

These aspects of the voice are what actor-academics, Robert Barton and Rocco Dal Vera, refer to as the 'voice recipe'. We will look at these 'ingredients' separately, with exercises adapted from Barton and Dal Vera (2017).

The different aspects of your voice

Think of a sentence that you might say, perhaps in a teaching context. If it helps, write the sentence down so that you can practise saying it aloud. Reflect on the following aspects of your voice[1], and think about how you would apply each aspect to your chosen sentence.

Tempo describes the rate of your speech, that is, how quickly or slowly you speak. This is about the extent to which the tempo remains steady throughout a sentence. You might also identify circumstances which seem to cause your tempo to increase, such as being excited or nervous.

Rhythm describes the patterns of beats in your voice. You might identify particular words or parts of sentences where you tend to place stress and emphasis, or there might be a pattern to where you tend to pause when you are speaking.

---

[1] The terms used to describe the various aspects of the voice are Barton and Dal Vera's terms (2017: 23-25).

Articulation describes how clearly you produce the sounds of each word – also referred to as diction. This is not about volume or pronunciation; you could be speaking quite softly and even mispronounce words, and yet articulate the sounds very well. You may tend to mumble at certain points in a sentence, or you might combine particular sounds when you speak.

Pronunciation describes your accent and dialect. There are many accepted ways to pronounce words depending on standard and regional variations. Your pronunciation is about where the character and colour of your sounds fit within the expectations of the language. You may speak with 'standard' pronunciation or with a regional accent, or perhaps you speak English as an additional language (see below).

Pitch describes how high or low you tend to speak. You have already done an exercise to find your vocal range. If you recorded your voice in the exercise above, you may have found that your pitch was higher in reality than on the recording. You may also have noticed variations in your pitch, or perhaps you tend to speak using more or less the same notes.

Volume describes how loud your voice is. You may speak at a consistent volume or you might adapt the volume of your voice in response to the space you are in. When someone is speaking too quietly, they are often told to raise their voice. However, this can lead to an increase in pitch, which in turn can make the voice sound tense. The challenge is to increase the volume whilst maintaining a lower, calm pitch. It is important that all students are able to access the lesson, so appropriate volume is a key aspect of the voice. This not only means speaking loud enough, but also varying the volume depending on the stage of the session, for example lowering the volume when speaking with an individual or a small group, and increasing the volume in whole-class activities.

Quality describes the tone of your voice and the feelings it evokes in listeners. You can think about adjectives you might use to describe your voice, such as nasal, husky, velvety, creamy, rich, and weak. One way to consider the quality of your voice is to think about how it sounds – or how it changes – when you have a cold.

Word choice describes your vocabulary and the words you choose to convey your message. If you have a large vocabulary, you have access to a larger number of choices and are able to vary how you communicate. You might be able to identify words which you use frequently, or perhaps you tend to use certain idioms or slang terms often.

Vocal nonverbals, which we might also refer to as paralinguistic features, describe the sounds, noises, and idiosyncrasies that you use to accompany your speech. These might include fillers, such as umm... ahh..., audible sighs and exhalations, humming, clicking, (frequent) throat clearing, and (nervous) laughter. We often use these subconsciously so it is important to become more aware of how our vocal nonverbals might affect (positively or negatively) our communication with our students.

Exercise: describing your voice

Reflect on each of the aspects of your voice using the prompt questions in Table 4.1. Try to describe and characterise your voice. You might find it helpful to think of (or write down) a sentence to illustrate each of the aspects of your voice.

Reflecting on the different aspects of your voice will help you to gain a sense of your voice's character and scope, and you may be able to identify features of your voice that can be developed. For example, you may discover that you have quite a large vocal range, but that you tend to use only a very narrow range when you speak. Or perhaps you will identify certain sound clusters that are difficult for you to articulate. Or maybe you will realise that you tend to speak too fast. From your reflections, try to highlight two or three aspects of your voice that you would like to improve. Make a note of these and bear them in mind in the next exercise. This increased self-awareness will also enable you to help your students to follow a similar process.

Exercise: experimenting with your voice

> So one thing that comes to mind immediately is the ability to throw and vary your voice – especially as a singer. When people describe bad teachers, they often talk about teachers with monotonous voices. So being able to control and vary the dynamics of your voice is a huge part of teaching.
>
> James Marples, Interview 7

From the previous exercise, keep in mind the two or three aspects of your voice that you feel require some development. Then practise reading the text below, focusing on the different aspects of voice in Table 4.1 It may help to focus on one or two aspects at a time. The text below is

67

■ TABLE 4.1 Describing your voice (adapted from Barton & Dal Vera 2017: 23–25)

Voice aspect	Reflections
Tempo	How would you describe your rate of speech? Do you tend to speak faster or slower than other people? Can you identify any patterns in your rate of speech? Do you tend to speed up or slow down at particular points in a sentence?
Rhythm	Think of your voice as a song. How would you describe the rhythm of your voice; the beats of the music in your voice? Where do you tend to place stress and emphasis in a sentence? Do you emphasise particular parts of sentences, or particular words; particular sounds? Do you tend to pause at particular points in a sentence? Do you do this for a conscious reason or is it an unconscious habit?
Articulation	How would you describe your articulation? Do you speak with very clear, crisp diction, with clearly discernible sounds? Or do you slur sounds or mumble particular parts of sentences? Can you identify any sounds that you find difficult to articulate? Do you avoid using certain words or sounds because you have identified that you find it hard to articulate them? How clearly do you articulate consonants? Can you clearly hear a difference between, for example, /t/ and /d/ or /b/ and /p/?
Pronunciation	How would you describe your pronunciation; your accent? Do you speak English with 'standard' pronunciation? Do you have a regional accent? Do you speak English as an additional language? Do sounds from your first language (or other languages that you speak) influence your pronunciation in English?
Pitch	Where would you place your normal speaking voice compared to other people? Is it lower? Higher? Think back to the exercise where you were finding your vocal range. How would you describe your voice in singing terms? Are you a soprano? A tenor? A bass? Can you identify parts of your vocal range that you use frequently and parts that you use less frequently? Could you use more of your range to produce a more varied sound? Do you tend to end sentences on rising or falling intonation, that is, does it often sound like you are asking a question or making a statement?

▥ TABLE 4.1 (continued)

Voice aspect	Reflections
Volume	How loud is your normal speaking voice compared to other people? How easy do you find it to adapt the volume of your voice to the space you are in? Can you easily increase the volume (without raising the pitch) to speak louder? Can you easily decrease the volume (without decreasing the quality) to speak more quietly?
Quality	How would you describe the tone and character of your voice? How do you think others perceive your voice? Has anyone ever commented on the sound and tone of your voice? Is it described as soothing, nasal, booming, husky...? How would you like your voice to sound? Is there a tone and quality of another person's voice that you would like to imitate?
Word choice	How would you describe your range of vocabulary? Can you easily find words to articulate what you want to say? To what extent does your vocabulary differ when you are teaching compared to day-to-day life? Do you tend to use any particular idiomatic language or slang terms? Can you identify any words that you seem to use very frequently?
Vocal nonverbals	Which nonverbals do you tend to use most frequently? These are idiosyncratic – unique to you – such as deep, audible inhalation when you are pausing and thinking; noises to fill pauses, such as *umm... ahh...*, and so on. What are the reasons for using these vocal nonverbals? Are they just unconscious habits? Do you use them when you are nervous? Do you use particular ones for particular reasons?

an extract from the beginning of Franz Kafka's novella, *Metamorphosis* (*Die Verwandlung*), translated from German into English by David Wyllie. If you prefer, you can choose a different text, or write a piece of your own, perhaps from course or lecture notes that you use when you teach. The text itself is not of particular importance; the text simply enables you to experiment with your voice and delivery. Record yourself reading the passage by Kafka (or a passage of your choice) in the following ways:

1   Read the passage aloud in your usual speaking voice without thinking too much initially. Listen back to the recording

and focus in particular on the aspects that you would like to improve. For example, if you are focusing on tempo, what is your basic rate of speech? Do you speak too quickly or too slowly? Do you speed up or slow down at particular points?

2   Read the passage again, this time experimenting with your vocal range. Read one sentence by saying each word on the same note. Then change to a different note on the next sentence. Experiment with notes at the higher and lower ends of your range.

3   Having experimented with pitch, now focus on the rhythm and musicality of the words you are reading. This time, *sing* the passage! It may feel awkward at first, but do it anyway. You are the only person listening. Let go of your inhibitions and allow a tune to carry the words. Don't think about it too much; just sing the passage, varying pitch, volume, tempo…

4   Listen back to the recordings, focusing in particular on the first and the third recordings. Can you identify any differences or improvements? Are there any sounds or words which were more difficult to articulate when you were speaking, compared with when you were singing?

5   Read the passage a final time. Before you start recording, identify at least two aspects of your voice that you will change in order to deliver the text. Listen back to the final recording. Do you notice any improvements compared to the first recording?

Extract from *Metamorphosis*[2]

One morning, when Gregor Samsa woke from troubled dreams, he found himself transformed in his bed into a horrible vermin. He lay on his armour-like back, and if he lifted his head a little he could see his brown belly, slightly domed and divided by arches into stiff sections. The bedding was hardly able to cover it and seemed ready to slide off any moment. His many legs, pitifully thin compared with the size of the rest of him, waved about helplessly as he looked.

"What's happened to me?" he thought. It wasn't a dream. His room, a proper human room although a little too small, lay

---

[2] By Franz Kafka, translated by David Wyllie. Project Gutenberg https://www.gutenberg.org/files/5200/5200-h/5200-h.htm (Retrieved 31 December 2019).

peacefully between its four familiar walls. A collection of textile samples lay spread out on the table – Samsa was a travelling salesman – and above it there hung a picture that he had recently cut out of an illustrated magazine and housed in a nice, gilded frame. It showed a lady fitted out with a fur hat and fur boa who sat upright, raising a heavy fur muff that covered the whole of her lower arm towards the viewer.

This exercise helps to make you more consciously aware of how you are speaking and how you are using your voice to help (or hinder) the delivery of the message. Singing the text helps you to shift your attention away from the words and focus instead on presentation and the different ingredients of your voice. Try this exercise using different passages, including real passages from your teaching context, and focus on different elements of your voice each time.

LINGUISTIC EXPRESSION AND PRONUNCIATION

In Chapter 1, we looked at some of the common performance anxieties experienced by new teachers in higher education. Two of these relate to clear communication, and more specifically, pronunciation and linguistic expression, particularly when tasked with teaching in a second language. Whilst this is a legitimate concern, it is also important to say that we all have a unique way of speaking, and our accent is part of our identity, so we should not strive to speak in one particular way or with one particular accent. Specifically in the context of actor training, McAllister-Viel (2019) highlights the increasing multicultural and multilingual context in which actors learn their craft, and so different voices ought to be celebrated. The same can be said of teaching.

Having said this, as we saw in Table 1.1, some new teachers are often concerned about their level of English expression and their accent in English, so it is important to offer support where it is needed and/or wanted. In my experience, these concerns are often raised by teachers whose first language is not English (L2 English speakers). However, I have also spoken to teachers who speak English as their first (and sometimes only) language (L1 English speakers), for whom English expression and pronunciation, particularly accent, is sometimes a concern. Some of the exercises in this section are of particular relevance to L2 English speakers; however, the techniques are also useful to any teacher, regardless of their first language. In fact, L1 English speakers can often benefit from practising pronunciation and articulation techniques. L1 English speakers have learned the language from birth, largely passively, so it is useful to raise awareness of the sounds you are making and how you are distinguishing (or not!) between the sounds you are making.

> During my first year [of teaching], I had a thing about whether they [the students] could understand my accent, and that was making me even more anxious at times. Or the fact that I couldn't get really heavy accents [...]. I cannot be less Greek; I am thinking in Greek; I think the structure of my sentences is different really because the Greek language is very visual. It has a very rich vocabulary. I was saying to the students – you don't need any subtext because the words are so heavy, but with English there is a lot of subtext and sometimes I don't understand the subtext, and that's a barrier for me with my students as well [...] I mean if you want to discuss in theatre terms – the fourth wall is there because of the subtext, you know, so my worry is trying to pull that wall down for them. [...] Yeah, for sure, the language thing was a big thing for me in the beginning, really big and made me really anxious.
>
> Sofia Alexiadou, Interview 1

Exercise: minimal pairs

Minimal pairs are pairs of words that vary by only one sound. These can be the source of pronunciation difficulties, such as /f/ in free versus /θ/ in three, or /ɪ/ in ship versus /iː/ in sheep, or /l/ in alive versus /r/ in arrive. It can help your pronunciation and your articulation if you focus on how you produce the sounds in the minimal pairs. Try articulating the following minimal pairs, paying attention to the shape of your mouth and lips, and the position of your tongue. Try to produce a crisp, strong sound as you articulate each pair of sounds. It might help to stand in front of a mirror so that you can see how the shape of your mouth and lips changes as you pronounce the alternative sound in each pair. You could also record yourself so that you can review your progress. For L2 English speakers, this exercise can help with pronunciation in particular. For L1 English speakers, this exercise is perhaps more useful in practising clear, crisp articulation of the consonants.

1   /ɪ/ in ship versus /iː/ in sheep
2   /ɪ/ in sit versus /iː/ in seat

3 /ɪ/ in chip versus /iː/ in cheap
4 /f/ in fast versus /p/ in past
5 /g/ in ghost versus /k/ in coast
6 /p/ in pie versus /t/ in tie
7 /t/ in tie versus /d/ in die
8 /æ/ in bad versus /e/ in bed
9 /æ/ in bat versus /ʌ/ in but
10 /ʃ/ in shore versus /tʃ/ in chore
11 /s/ in see versus /ʃ/ in she
12 /θ/ in breath versus /ð/ in breathe
13 **/s/** in sink versus /θ/ in think
14 /ð/ in with versus /z/ in whizz
15 /z/ in faze versus /s/ in face
16 /d/ in bad versus /dʒ/ in badge
17 /d/ in hard versus /t/ in heart
18 /aɪ/ in ride versus /eɪ/ in raid
19 /ɒ/ in got versus /əʊ/ in goat
20 /eə/ in hair versus /ɜː/ in her

Isolating minimal pairs helps you to practise articulating two similar sounds. The next step is to put these sounds into words and phrases so that you can practise producing clear articulation of potentially problematic sounds in context.

Exercise: articulation drills

Improving your articulation will mean that your voice will be more audible – it will be heard more easily – and it will be more intelligible – listeners will be able to distinguish between the different sounds you are producing. We often confuse volume with articulation. This is illustrated when someone tells you to "speak up!" They probably can actually *hear* you, but they cannot *understand* you. This is a problem with articulation and diction, not volume. When we become highly competent in the language, whether we speak the language as our first language or not, we can become lazy in our articulation and formation of the various sounds in the language. Articulation drills can help to remind us of the complexities of the language and increase our awareness of the importance of clear diction.

The articulation drills here are adapted from Barton and Dal Vera (2017: 81–84). Practise saying each phrase, focusing on producing crisp, clear, distinct sounds. Challenge yourself to say each phrase as many times as you can in one breath. Record yourself so that you can review how clearly you are articulating the words and phrases.

1 Abominable abdominals
2 Angry banker anchored in Bangor
3 Begging beguilingly
4 Choose orange shoes
5 Dapper dabber
6 Literally literary
7 Depth and breadth
8 Did you, would you, could you
9 Don't you, won't you, can't you
10 Fixed perspectives
11 Mixed biscuits
12 Lemon liniment
13 Eleven benevolent elephants
14 Heather's hat has ten thousand feathers
15 Eight great grey geese grazing gaily in Greece
16 Martin met a mob of marching munching monkeys
17 Three tethered teething things
18 The thorn had torn through
19 While her withers wither with her
20 Wicked wicket victim

Foreign language accent imitation

Another interesting exercise, which in some ways involves acting, is foreign language accent imitation. This can be useful for teachers who use English as an additional language, but there is also evidence that this technique can be beneficial for L1 English speakers. In essence, the technique consists of speaking the first language (L1) with an imitated accent of another language (L2). For example, imagine a teacher from Germany is teaching at an English-speaking university. She would speak German, but she would try to imitate the sounds and expression of English in the German words and sentences. I have personally tried this in reverse. I am a speaker of German (L2) but my first language (L1) is English. Not only is it fun, but it also allows you to focus exclusively on your accent in the other language (L2). As you are speaking your L1, you do not have to concentrate on producing correct syntax and grammar in the L2.

A study in the Polish context involved students of English (L1 Polish; L2 English) imitating English sounds while speaking Polish. In this research, Rojczyk (2015) showed that students were able to isolate key differences between Polish and English sounds, helping to highlight aspects of the L2 (English) accent which were, perhaps to some extent subconsciously, already internalised by the Polish speakers. Once this awareness has been raised, the sounds and accentual differences identified can be practised again in the L2, in this case English.

This technique is not only for teachers who are teaching in a second language, however. Some researchers have used similar exercises to highlight accentual differences within the same language. Adank et al. (2013), for example, asked first-language English speakers (from England) to listen to two Scottish speakers, each speaking with a Glaswegian accent. The research participants were asked simply to repeat in their own English accent the sentences spoken by one of the Glaswegian speakers. Then they were asked to imitate the accent of the other Glaswegian speaker. The imitation phase of the experiment resulted in positive perceptions of the speaker's social attractiveness. This suggests that by *acting* like the speaker, the listener experiences greater empathy and develops a more positive perception of the speaker.

The potential benefit of this exercise is the heightened awareness about the sounds and melody of the language. If English is not your first language, foreign language accent imitation can help you to recognise the salient sounds of English so that you can pay particular attention to these when you are speaking English. If English is your first language, a focus on a different accent can help to highlight the variation that exists, dialectically and phonetically, in the language, so that you can start to vary your intonation, for example.

QUICK IMITATION EXERCISE:

If English is not your first language, take a paragraph from a book in your first language and read it using the sounds of English. If it helps, imagine how an English speaker would pronounce your language. As you read, notice the salient sounds. What are the main differences in consonant and vowel sounds? What are the main intonation differences?

If English is your first language, choose a regional accent that you do not know well, perhaps from a different region or from a different English-speaking country. Listen to the accent, perhaps from a video online. Then

---

75

read a passage in English, trying to imitate the sounds of the accent you have chosen. What are the salient differences in consonant and vowel sounds? Are there any differences in intonation? Could you use any of these differences to make your own voice more varied, rich, and interesting when speaking in your own accent?

VOICE PROJECTION

Another important aspect of the voice is projection, which is more than just increasing the volume. If you have ever been told "Speak up! I can't hear you", it is likely that you became anxious and simply tried to speak louder. We know from previous discussions about breathing that nervousness can affect how we breathe. Fast, shallow breathing has a negative impact on the sound and quality of the voice. Simply trying to speak louder, or shouting, does not help to project the voice, and it is also not a healthy way to increase the volume of your voice.

Exercise: posture

An important factor in projecting your voice is posture. If you have 'bad' posture, with a closed, slouching frame, your chest will be constricted and will impede your voice's exit from your body. You can check your posture, and its relation to voice projection, with a simple counting exercise. In order to compare your voice before and after, you may find it useful to record yourself.

1   Stand comfortably but with slouching posture, shoulders slightly rounded. Take a deep breath, supported from your diaphragm. Count upwards from one in your normal speaking voice. Count as high as you can in one breath.
2   Place one hand on your sternum between the two halves of your rib cage. Repeat the counting exercise, slowly lifting your sternum, opening up your posture.
3   Repeat this a few times, noticing how the sound of your voice changes. Find the posture that is comfortable and that allows your voice to project without working the throat too hard.
4   If you were recording yourself, listen to the recordings and see if you can hear a difference in the resonance and projection of your voice when you started to open your posture.

Exercise: resonance

As we saw at the beginning of this chapter, speech sounds are created by articulation. The vibrations which start from the vocal folds can then be made more resonant, which increases volume. A resonant voice has more volume, but the speaker is not working harder. Singers sometimes talk about forward placement and singing in the masque, focusing the voice in the upper-front part of the face where a mask might be worn. This can be useful for thinking about increasing the resonance of your voice. You can start to feel the resonance of your voice by doing a simple humming exercise.

1   Start by humming at a pitch that feels comfortable. Play around with the hum until you feel the vibrations resonating on your lips.
2   When you can feel your lips vibrating, slowly open your mouth and work through the vowels. Check the resonance on the lips at regular intervals.
3   The exercise goes like this: hum-vowel-hum-vowel-hum-vowel.
4   mmmAHHmmmAHHmmm.
5   mmmEEEmmmEEEmmm.
6   mmmOHHmmmOHHmmm.
7   mmmOOOmmmOOOmmm.

The resonance from your lips during the hum (mmm) should carry through into the vowel sound. You can also try variations of this. For example, you could try counting upwards with a hum before each number:

mmmONE; mmmTWO; mmmTHREE; mmmFOUR; mmmFIVE; mmmSIX

The aim is to become aware of the vibrations in your mouth and face and to feed this resonance into the sounds you produce. However, as we discussed earlier in this chapter, the resonance (the vibrations) does not come from the face, the lips, the bones, etc. The vibrations begin in our vocal folds. The vibrations you feel in your bones and your lips are so-called sympathetic vibrations, or sympathetic resonance. A good example of this can be seen on many musical instruments, such as the violin. On a violin, the second string from the left is a D (see Figure 4.2). The next string along is an A. If the violinist plays the A-string with her third finger on the string, she will be playing a D at one octave higher than the D on the string next to it. The D-string will resonate

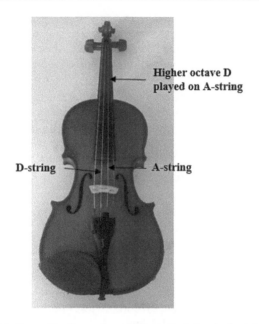

Higher octave D
played on A-string

D-string

A-string

FIGURE 4.2 Sympathetic resonance from D-string to A-string
on the violin

'in sympathy' with the vibrations created by the note played on the
A-string, creating a ringing, richer, more resonant sound.

A similar phenomenon occurs when we use our voice. The vocal
folds are the source of the vibrations and, depending on the pitch,
other parts of our vocal anatomy, such as the bones in our face and
our lips, vibrate too, and these vibrations can help us to make a more
resonant sound. In this way, the voice is not necessarily louder, but
it is projected outwards. By allowing the voice to be carried on these
vibrations, we are able to create more resonance without necessarily
putting in more effort. This is important for keeping the voice strong
and healthy.

CARING FOR YOUR VOICE

We started this chapter by saying that the voice is one of the most
important tools a teacher uses. It is likely that you have experienced
some form of voice fatigue at some point in your career, but we tend
not to worry too much unless we develop a more serious condition.

Clare Chandler makes an interesting point about workshops and training in vocal health for performers:

> "Teachers can experience lots of vocal issues because of misusing their instrument. Performers spend lots of time on vocal training and yet within teaching practice, you rarely find sessions in teacher training on vocal health."
>
> Clare Chandler, Interview 10

In teacher training at primary and secondary level, sessions on vocal health are often included as part of routine training. However, as Clare Chandler notes, this rarely seems to transfer to the higher education teaching context. This is perhaps an area of training that needs to be developed, especially if we agree that teaching shares many similarities with performance.

The factors and exercises discussed in this chapter help to raise awareness of the voice. This awareness alone can go a long way to helping to keep the voice healthy. This said, there are several, perhaps obvious, behaviours and habits that should be highlighted, as they can contribute to deterioration of the voice:

- smoking and exposure to fumes and toxins that can affect breathing
- lack of fluids – simply forgetting to drink water little and often
- speaking at excessive volume, and shouting, rather than developing a resonant voice
- excessive throat clearing and coughing
- lack of warm up for the voice
- poor breathing technique – shallow, chest breathing rather than deep, supported, diaphragmatic breathing

Some of the techniques presented in this chapter and in Chapter 3, particularly good breathing technique, can help you to maintain a healthy voice. Performers sometimes also use a variety of self-treatments, such as inhaling hot steam or gargling with salt water. These may be helpful, but the key to long-term good voice health is to practise using your voice in a safe way. Some of the exercises presented here, and in other books, may not work for you straight away. It is a matter of practising for short periods of time, but frequently. The voice is the audible part of the teacher's performance, and this is accompanied by the body, which is the focus of our next chapter.

REFERENCES AND FURTHER READING

Adank, P., Stewart, A. J., Connell, L., & Wood, J. (2013) Accent imitation positively affects language attitudes. *Frontiers in Psychology* 4, 1–10.

Barton, R. & Dal Vera, R. (2017) *Voice onstage and off*, 3rd ed. New York: Routledge.

Berry, C. (1991) *Voice and the actor*, Revised ed. New York: Wiley.

Berry, C. (2000) *Your voice and how to use it*, Revised ed. London: Virgin.

Calais-German, B. & German, F. (2016) *Anatomy of voice. How to enhance and project your best voice.* Vermont: Healing Arts Press.

Friedlander, C. (2018) *Complete vocal fitness. A singer's guide to physical training, anatomy and biomechanics.* London: Rowman & Littlefield.

Hughes, S. M. & Harrison, M. A. (2013) I like my voice better: Self-enhancement bias in perceptions of voice attractiveness. *Perception* 42, 941–949.

Linklater, K. (2006) *Freeing the natural voice. Imagery and art in the practice of voice and language*, Revised ed. London: Nick Hern.

McAllister-Viel, T. (2019) *Training actors' voices: Towards and intercultural/interdisciplinary approach.* Oxford: Routledge.

Rodenburg, P. (2002) *The actor speaks: Voice and the performer.* Basingstoke: Palgrave Macmillan.

Rodenburg, P. (2015) *The right to speak: Working with the voice*, 2nd ed. London: Bloomsbury.

Rojczyk, A. (2015) Using FL accent imitation in L1 in foreign-language speech research. In: E. Waniek-Klimczak & M. Pawlak (eds.) *Teaching and researching the pronunciation of English.* Heidelberg: Springer, 223–234.

Chapter 5

The body

> "I purposely use my body in my lecture. I am a wandering lecturer anyway, so I try to use the motions of my body to express the enthusiasm I have for my content."
>
> **Megan Bylsma, Interview 8**

In the last chapter, we explored various aspects of the voice, which we said is one of the most important instruments at a teacher's disposal. The other key instrument, or perhaps vessel, is the body. While the voice resides inside the body, and can be trained to make an impact externally, the body itself is visible and constantly on display to the audience – or students – and so the body cannot be overlooked when considering performative aspects of teaching. Our considerations of the voice focused on vocal performance, and now we turn our attention to the teacher's visual performance.

The lecture format, in particular, places the teacher in the spotlight and is perhaps closest to some of the notions of performance outlined in Chapter 1, such as standing on a stage and speaking in front of an audience. If you have or have had the opportunity to attend a microteaching session or have your teaching filmed (Chapter 2), you can start to assess your own visual performance by reflecting on some of the topics discussed in this chapter. We start here by looking briefly at lecturing and presenting, as the teacher is particularly visible during these two activities.

A NOTE ON LECTURING AND PRESENTING

> I think the most obvious way that teaching is performance are the moments when you're 'sage on the stage' and people are looking at you; it feels like a performance.
>
> Lindsay Masland, Interview 2

The notion of a 'sage on the stage' evokes images of a professor giving a lecture to a packed auditorium, with students listening passively while the lecture is 'performed', or in some cases read aloud from a script. The fact that academics are called 'lecturers' (and 'readers' for some higher ranking academics in the UK) illustrates the traditionally didactic nature of teaching in higher education, with transmission of knowledge from teacher to students. These job titles stem from the Latin *lectitare* – to be in the habit of reading. This focus on 'reading' perhaps takes our focus away from active learning and the importance of students being actively involved in the learning process. However, as many teachers still teach in large lecture formats, it is important for us to consider this teaching space when discussing performance.

As academics and teachers in higher education, we might be quite used to giving presentations at conferences or at faculty meetings. But how does presenting differ from lecturing? Perhaps it is easier to start by thinking about what these two contexts have in common: structure and storytelling. A good presentation or a good lecture is well-structured with clear signposting between the constituent parts. The performative aspect of this comes in the form of storytelling: taking the audience on a journey and bringing the subject matter to life with interesting and relevant examples. Where presenting and lecturing begin to diverge is when we start thinking about interactions between the audience (or students) and the presenter (or teacher). As discussed in Chapter 7, there is now more emphasis on active learning in higher education. This means we have far more interactivity in our classes, including in lectures, and the 'sage on the stage' figure is no longer the only 'performer' in the room. This raises questions about how we perform, visually, when we are leading a large lecture – as well as when we are in smaller teaching spaces; how we use our body to communicate, to engage and to stimulate (inter)activity. We will look at this first by getting to know our bodies, and then by drawing inspiration from the worlds of acting and dance.

GETTING TO KNOW YOUR BODY

In Chapter 4, we spent some time getting to know our voices, starting by *confronting* the reality of how our voices sound in our heads compared with how they sound to an objective ear, when recorded. It is useful to do a similar exercise in relation to the body. You can do this by reviewing recent footage of yourself in a teaching or a presenting scenario – such as a microteaching session, as discussed in Chapter 2.

QUICK BODY CHECK:

If available, take a recent video recording of yourself in a teaching or a presenting scenario. Alternatively, you could record yourself briefly using your phone or any other video recording device, though it will be more realistic and valuable if you can arrange to be recorded in a 'real' situation. Watch the footage and focus on your visual performance; your body. How do you look? How is your posture? Do you use any particular gestures frequently? Do you move around in the teaching/presenting space? Do you maintain eye contact with anyone in the audience? Do you like what you see on the recording?

THE DIFFERENT ASPECTS OF YOUR BODY

Being mindful of my breathing and how my body is feeling was highly developed through dance. Dance often involves holding a position and then releasing. So when I recognise that I am holding tension in my body, I can locate it and release it almost as a matter of habit. Using the teaching arena like a stage by moving/changing positions while I am lecturing or tutoring is helpful too.

(Susan Maloney, Interview 5)

In the last chapter, we looked at different aspects of the voice, drawing on Barton and Dal Vera's (2017) work in actor training. Here, we apply a similar approach to the body, drawing again on actor-academic, Robert Barton who, together with academic and performer, Barbara Sellers-Young, has written about the importance of performers understanding their bodies. In this section, we explore different aspects of the body, adapting Barton and Sellers-Young's (2017) 'body recipe'[1] to the teaching context. As you read through the following (Table 5.1), picture yourself in a teaching scenario, perhaps giving a lecture in a large auditorium, or leading a tutorial in front of a group of students. Think about your responses to the prompt questions when you are in your chosen imagined scenario.

By reflecting on the aspects of your body in Table 5.1, you can start to get a picture of how you appear, visually, to others when

[1] The terms used to describe the various aspects of the body are Barton and Sellers-Young's terms (2017: 4-8).

TABLE 5.1 Describing your body (adapted from Barton & Sellers-Young 2017: 4–8)

Body aspect	Reflections
Standing	How do you stand? How is your weight distributed? Is your weight evenly distributed across both legs, or more on one leg than the other?
	How is your posture? Do you stand very upright? Do you tend to slouch or lean to one side? How symmetrical are you?
Sitting	Do you often sit when you are teaching?
	How is your posture when you are sitting? Do you tend to sit upright, or do you sink into the chair?
	What is a comfortable sitting position for you? Do you tend to cross your arms or legs?
Expression	What is the usual expression on your face? What are your three most common expressions? Have other people told you that you look a particular way when you are speaking or listening?
	Do you maintain eye contact with others? Do you 'scan' the room to catch the eyes of different students?
	Do your facial expressions change naturally, or are you aware of consciously changing your expressions in order to show the reactions you think your students expect, e.g. widening the eyes to express surprise; smiling to acknowledge an excellent response from a student?
	Do any other parts of your face tend to communicate what you are thinking, e.g. do your eyebrows move; do you frown; do you purse your lips?
Tempo/Rhythm	Do you tend to move around the teaching space? Are your movements fast or slow? What is your basic rate of movement?
	Do you tend to make any sudden movements or do you move in a considered way?
Motion	Is there noticeable preparation before you move, e.g. if you are sitting, do you lean back first, take a deep breath and show that you are about to move or stand? If you are standing, do you shift your weight from one leg to the other before you start walking, or is the transition from standing to walking smooth?
	Do you tend to move quite freely, or do you use objects near to you for support as you move, such as running your hand along a table as you move around the classroom?

TABLE 5.1 (continued)

Body aspect	Reflections
Gestures	How would you describe your body language? Do you tend to keep your arms close to your body, or do your arms and hands move quite freely?
	To what extent do you use gestures unconsciously? Try sitting on your hands while you speak. Is this easy, or do you feel the need to use your hands and arms to help you communicate?
	Can you identify any gestures that are idiosyncratic and unique to you? Do others make gestures that you would like to incorporate into your own movements?
	To what extent do your gestures help to communicate your thoughts and feelings? Could someone follow the key message without hearing your voice?
Adaptations	How do your movements change in different situations?
	How do your movements change if you are feeling stressed or if you are experiencing performance anxiety?
	How do your movements change depending on the teaching space, e.g. in a large lecture theatre versus a small seminar room?
Cultural binding	To what extent do your movements reveal that you are part of a particular group or culture? Do you move/gesture in similar ways to close friends or people in your family?
	To what extent do your movements indicate that you are a scholar, an academic, or a teacher? Are you aware that you use your body in certain ways based on teachers, academics, or performers who you have observed in the past?
Mannerisms	Can you identify any idiosyncratic, subconscious quirks in your body or movements? Do you have any mannerisms that surface when you are stressed?
	Does your head move to emphasise key words? Do you nod enthusiastically when a student is answering a question?
	Do you fiddle with a ring on your finger when you are thinking? Do you run your hand through your hair at particular times when you are speaking?
	How would others describe your mannerisms? What would an observer pick out as mannerisms that are typical of you?

performing in the teacher role. Reflect on the extent to which any of your movements help or hinder communication of your message, and the extent to which your body and your movements enhance your visual performance. Is there anything that you would like to develop further? Or is there anything that you would like to stop doing? For example, perhaps you have identified gestures that are distracting; gestures that do not help to communicate what you are trying to say. Or perhaps you would like to improve your posture so that you appear more open and upright. From your reflections, try to highlight two or three aspects of your visual performance that could be enhanced.

GESTURES, BODY LANGUAGE, AND POSTURE

From Table 5.1, gestures stand out as an aspect of the body worthy of further consideration in the context of teaching. More broadly, body language plays an important part in communication and in the visual performance of a teacher. A frequently cited figure is that only 7% of communication is verbal, while 93% of communication is nonverbal. In reality, it is not possible to say with such accuracy how much of human communication is verbal or nonverbal. Human behaviour and communication are complex and messy, and the 7%/93% figures, which were originally introduced by Albert Mehrabian (1981), are often applied incorrectly. Nevertheless, it certainly is the case that nonverbal aspects of communication are vital and need to be considered carefully in teaching performance. In Chapter 1, we saw how gestures can be used to reinforce students' learning. The example given there was the so-called *nobjects* study, where learning was shown to be enhanced by combining specific gestures with the learning of particular words. In addition to aiding students' learning, gestures and body language also have an impact on visual performance, and can influence how you are perceived by your students. In interview 3, Kate Nasser offered her thoughts on body language in her work as a coach and a public speaker:

> "I am big on body language but not all my body language is big. When you let your natural body language emerge, it communicates so much more than words. On the other hand, if you 'learn' body language, it may seem fake. Also, if all your body language is big and bold, people become numb to it."
>
> (Kate Nasser, Interview 3)

Kate Nasser raises the important issue of authenticity. In Chapter 1, I started by saying that I do not consider teaching to be acting. This is echoed in Kate Nasser's quote: body language can aid communication but, as a teacher, any use of nonverbal communication must come across as 'natural' and authentic. There also needs to be sufficient variation so that students do not become overwhelmed by consistently very big gestures, or bored by a lack of gestures.

Gestures might also include not just movements of particular parts of the body, but actually moving the whole body, in a planned and intentional way, to help communicate a certain point. In Interview 2, Lindsay Masland talked about some of the skills she uses from her experience in dance and musical theatre to help with storytelling in higher education teaching:

> "in terms of specific things I'm doing: ... thinking about where I'm standing when I'm saying certain things; thinking about it all in stories."
>
> (Lindsay Masland, Interview 2)

So movements around the teaching space might be spontaneous and unplanned, but it is also useful to try planning some very intentional moves. For example, to emphasise two diametrically opposed ideas or concepts, it might help to move to a diametrically opposite part of the room when introducing the opposing concept. David Jay in Interview 4 has conducted research on the use of numbered shorthand for teacher positions in the classroom, for example, which he adapted from classical dance where set positions, such as 1st position, 2nd position and so on, are commonplace (Jay 2018). Jay found that it can be helpful for the teacher to assign a numbered shorthand to different positions and to use these when planning lessons. For example, 1st position might refer to the teacher standing at the front of the room, in a standing position addressing the whole class; 2nd position might refer to the teacher being among the students during group work, with the body in a low position enabling closer interaction with a smaller group of students. Jay (2018) found that such intentional and planned positions were particularly helpful for new teachers.

Context, context, context

It is important to contextualise body language. We often hear, for example, that 'crossed arms' means the person is bored, angry, defensive – a negative emotion. This may be the case, but it is too simplistic to make this assumption. The person may simply be relaxed and comfortable and, for them, crossed arms may be a default, relaxed position. Think about your own body language in a variety of situations. If you are sitting with your arms crossed, does this always mean you are bored or disengaged? As teachers, we have the luxury of getting to know our students and, over time, we can start to understand their body language in more nuanced ways.

We also need to consider cultural differences in body language. For example, the use of arm and hand gestures are indispensable in some cultures, such as Italian and Spanish, but tend to be used less in others, such as in Nordic countries. We therefore need to be careful when interpreting others' body language, and try to adapt our own body language to our audience – students.

> And one more thing as a performer is to be aware of any unconscious tics, gestures or movements that you do that can be distracting to the audience. And I guess that's the same for teachers. So becoming aware of your body and body movements is really important.
>
> (James Marples, Interview 7)

Exercise: intentional gestures

In Table 5.1, there was a question about intentionality in your use of gestures; to what extent you use gestures subconsciously or in a planned way. Barton and Sellers-Young (2017) suggest sitting on your hands to force a more considered use of your hands when speaking. I often used this technique when teaching students of interpreting. Interpreters often have to stand in front of large groups of people, sometimes at high profile conferences and summits, and translate live, on the spot, from one language into another. A useful exercise in using hand gestures in a more intentional way is to try sitting on your hands while you speak.

1   Take a passage from one of your lectures or tutorials. Alternatively, use the extract below from Emmeline Pankhurst's 'Freedom or Death' speech, which she delivered on 13 November 1913 in Hartford, Connecticut.

> We wear no mark; we belong to every class; we permeate every class of the community from the highest to the lowest; and so you see in the woman's civil war the dear men of my country are discovering it is absolutely impossible to deal with it: you cannot locate it, and you cannot stop it.

> As long as women consent to be unjustly governed, they can be, but directly women say: "We withhold our consent, we will not be governed any longer so long as that government is unjust."

2   Sit on your hands and read out your chosen extract. How does it feel? Do you feel the urge to use hand gestures at certain times? Would these gestures serve any purpose or enhance the delivery of your message?

3   Think about gestures you might use with a particular purpose in mind. For example, in the Pankhurst speech, you might plan to use open hand and open arm gestures to emphasise 'every class', or perhaps move your hand from a high position to a low position when saying 'from the highest to the lowest'.

4   Deliver your extract again, this time with your hands free to gesture – but in a planned and an intentional way.

5   As an alternative, you could try speaking freely without reading from a script. This may be more challenging as it is likely to encourage more unconscious use of hand gestures.

Exercise: finding your base posture

Another important aspect of your body language relates to your posture – your overall frame and appearance in front of your students. In Table 5.1, you had an opportunity to reflect on how you stand, how you sit, and how your posture affects how you are perceived. A useful starting point here is to find your base posture – a comfortable, open posture where you feel and look relaxed.

1   Stand with your legs hips width apart.
2   Close your eyes.
3   Look up to the ceiling and raise your arms above your head, stretching the shoulders up and back.
4   Lower your arms to your sides and open your eyes.
5   This is your open, relaxed base posture.

Notice how this feels. Does it feel different to your usual posture? If you find yourself becoming visibly asymmetrical, or if you start to feel stiff or uncomfortable, it is helpful to remember how it feels to stand in this relaxed, open way.

An important technique to mention when considering posture is the Alexander Technique, which is a method of relaxing the body, reducing tension, and improving posture. The technique was developed by Frederick Matthias Alexander in the 1890s. At the time, Alexander was in the process of becoming an actor, but his progress was hindered by recurring vocal problems. He noticed that his problems stemmed from tension in his neck and head, and he spent the next few years developing techniques to reduce tension in his body. Nowadays, practitioners teach clients to become more aware of the body's movements, to move more efficiently and intentionally, and to improve their posture. The Alexander Technique is usually learned with a qualified practitioner, so we will not explore this further here. However, you can read more about the technique in the further reading at the end of this chapter, in Kelly McEvenue's book, *The Alexander Technique for Actors.*

INSIGHTS ABOUT MOVEMENT FROM ACTING AND DANCE

In the remainder of this chapter, we will explore some of the most influential movement practitioners in performance, including in acting and dance. We will look at some of the techniques and exercises used and suggest how these might be applied in the teaching context. We start by revisiting the work of Konstantin Stanislavski.

Re-educating your body and defining your motivation

In Chapter 3, we mentioned briefly the famous Russian actor and director, Konstantin Stanislavski. At the heart of the Stanislavski System is the importance of portraying a believable, natural character. Stanislavski's work is highly complex, and not all of it is necessarily relevant to the teaching context. However, an important concept is 're-education'. Stanislavski starts from the premise that being on a stage in front of an audience is not part of most people's everyday experience. In earlier approaches to theatre, actors would perform and gesture in over-the-top, grandiose ways which were not true-to-life. Stanislavski was radical in that he called for actors to speak and move in more natural ways. This is an interesting point for the teaching context. As we have already said, teachers are not actors; they are being (a version of) themselves, but in a performance space, such as a lecture theatre, we may need to re-educate ourselves so that our gestures, movements, and utterances can be seen and heard clearly without moving, shouting, or gesturing in an over-the-top, theatrical manner.

The other concept from Stanislavski of relevance here is 'motivation'. Lindsay Masland's quote above about intentional movements in the teaching space is an example of this. Stanislavski expected his actors to analyse every action and utterance of their characters: 'Why does the character move to the back of the stage at this point?' 'Why does the character tap her hands on the desk while she is talking?' By answering questions like these, the actor is showing that she/he is aware, on a deep level, of the character's motivations. Transferring this to the teaching context, a similar analysis of our own motivations can help us to make our movements and gestures more intentional and purposeful. If you watch a recording of yourself teaching (perhaps from a microteaching session – see Chapter 2), you can analyse your body language and your movements around the teaching space. Are you able to define your motivation for these movements and gestures? Do they help to emphasise a point? Are they distracting in any way? Or perhaps they are neutral, that is, they do not have a particular purpose but they also do not distract the students' attention. Either way, this can be a useful exercise to raise your awareness of how you use your body when you are teaching, and whether your movements are intentional or not.

We return to Stanislavski's work in Chapter 6 when we discuss another of his techniques – the magic if – to explore how this might be useful in relation to improvisation in teaching.

Stella Adler's Action

The famous American actress, Stella Adler, trained with Stanislavski in the 1930s. She developed her own approach, the Adler Technique, which emphasised *action* and *doing*. Adler trained actors to think not so much about emotions and feelings, but instead to think about what one character is doing to another. For example, if two characters are having an argument, Adler would ask the actors to act out their *actions* rather than their *feelings*. So rather than trying to portray anger, for example, she would ask the actors to analyse their actions, such as shouting at each other, pointing fingers at each other, moving towards each other, and so on. These actions and movements will also communicate the feeling – anger – but the actor's body and movements are foregrounded and the feelings and emotions are pushed to the background.

PAUSE FOR REFLECTION:

Imagine you are teaching a class and you notice two of your students near the back are being disruptive, chatting to each other, and talking over you. Think about how this might make you feel. Anxious? Angry? Indifferent? How would you communicate these feelings at that moment? Thinking in Adler's terms, what actions could you take? What gestures could you use in order to achieve your desired outcome – to encourage the students to stop their disruptive behaviour?

In the example above, the subtle shift in emphasis from feelings to actions could help the teacher to feel less anxious about the situation and to use physical presence in the teaching space to achieve the desired outcome. For example, the teacher could continue as normal but move towards the disruptive students; she/he could give an impromptu example, gesturing at one of the disruptive students, drawing them into the 'spotlight'.

More broadly, Adler's focus on actions – and our influence on others – helps us to keep the student at the centre of our attention. What actions do we want to take to help our students learn – pedagogically but also our physical actions in the classroom? This could be a helpful way of shifting the focus from the 'teacher as performer' onto the 'students as co-performers'. In some ways, this is in line with the prevalent outcomes-based approach to education: we create learning outcomes for our students and then we design activities to help them to achieve these outcomes.

Jacques Lecoq's mime and seven levels of tension

The famous French theatre director and teacher, Jacques Lecoq, emphasised the importance of physicality and the effective use of movement to aid communication. Lecoq established his own drama school in Paris in 1956 – the École internationale de theatre Jacques Lecoq – which trains students using a method called *mimodynamics*. Lecoq focused on the body, movements, and mime. According to Lecoq, mime is useful as it forces us to analyse movements, many of which may have become automatic and second nature over time. In relation to mime, Lecoq wrote:

> To mime is literally to embody and therefore to understand better ... miming is a way of rediscovering a thing with renewed freshness. The action of miming becomes a form of knowledge.
>
> (Lecoq 2000: 22)

It is doubtful that you carry out habitual movements consciously; you just move without thinking too much. It is similar when you think about how you move from one place to another. A good example of this is when somebody asks you for directions in the street: you may know very well how to go from point A to point B yourself, but it can be challenging to describe this sequence of moves to somebody else. For Lecoq, mime is a useful tool for making our movements more conscious and intentional.

Putting this into the context of teaching, we can think about how our body and our movements help (or hinder) our intended communication. We can also review some of the habitual movements we make in the classroom – either in our heads, by watching a video, or by miming some of these movements – in order to increase our awareness of our body.

Lecoq also developed his 'seven levels of tension', which aimed to connect the actor's emotions and body and enable the actor to communicate a variety of levels of tension using the body. The seven levels of tension are:

1   Exhausted or catatonic: there is no tension in the body, sometimes referred to as the jellyfish. Movement and speech require effort.
2   Laid back: movements are cool and relaxed, lacking in urgency or direction.
3   Neutral: you are present and aware, but there is no 'story' behind your movements. There is just the right amount of movement to communicate your message.
4   Alert: your movements display curiosity. There may also be indecision – looking around, sitting down, standing up, moving in one direction, then rethinking this and moving back again.
5   Suspense: the whole body is tense; the eyes also show tension. The movements you make when something is about to happen; a deep intake of breath and tensing of the muscles.
6   Passionate: the tension in the body is released, revealing emotions (anger, fear, etc.). Movements with this level of tension are difficult to control.
7   Tragic: the body is solid with tension. You are petrified.

Perhaps you can identify with some of these levels of tension. Some obvious scenarios might be lying on the sofa at the end of a long day, feeling exhausted (level 1), or hearing a noise in a dark room while you are sleeping, causing your body to become tense and your breathing to become fast and shallow (level 5). In everyday life, and in teaching, it is likely that levels one to four are most common, and perhaps levels three and four are most typical when we are teaching.

PAUSE FOR REFLECTION

Consider a teaching context where you are likely to be in a 'neutral' level of tension. For example, you are facilitating a discussion; you are moderating the discussion, prompting students to respond, making sure other students do not dominate the discussion. So you are present and aware, but your bodily movements are neutral. Think about any extraneous tension that might be visible in your body – tension and/or movements which are not required to fulfil your pedagogic aims. If possible, review video footage of a similar scenario to see if you can identify any tension or movements which are not 'neutral'.

The exercise above is useful for raising our awareness of excess, unnecessary tension. The next time you are in a teaching scenario like the one above – or any other scenario where you do not need to be tense or engaged in a lot of movement – try to become consciously aware of your body. For example, it is quite common to feel extraneous tension in the neck and shoulders, usually through raising the shoulders subconsciously and through taking in fast, shallow breaths.

Finally, and as has been mentioned several times, it is important to be intentional. It is not about prescribing how one person ought to move or use their body. Each person – each teacher – is an individual and must feel free to move in ways that feel natural, comfortable, and authentic. But by being aware of movements, and by using the body intentionally, you can start to use your body to help with communication. So just as we mentioned earlier about moving around the teaching space with intentionality, you could also plan to move through different levels of tension at different times, in order to emphasise or draw attention to particular points, or to create more energy in the room by moving at higher levels in Lecoq's scale.

Laban's Efforts

Perhaps one of the most well-known movement theorists and practitioners was Rudolf Laban. Laban was interested in expression through movement. He studied and observed human movement and compiled a large body of work which analysed, described, and interpreted how we move. One part of Laban's work, which is used by dancers and actors and which may be relevant to teachers, is his study of 'Efforts'. Laban's Efforts enable us to define the quality of movements; how a movement feels for us and for those observing us. Ewan and Sagovsky (2016) explain the relationship between movement and quality by comparing this with colour and light: different colours give light particular qualities, and we can use different colours in combination in order to create different shades. Likewise, we can use different Efforts to create different qualities of movement.

From his observations, Laban categorised movements according to the intention of the person carrying out the movement. He placed movements into four categories, each of which can be expressed with two opposing qualities. These are:

- Space/focus (direct or indirect)
- Time (quick or sustained)
- Weight (heavy or light)
- Flow (bound or free)

95

One common example to illustrate the different quality (effort) of the same movement is in extending one arm out in front of the body. The person might be expressing anger and their intention might be to hurt somebody, perhaps with a punching movement; or the person might intend to pick up an object, like a glass of water, which is placed somewhere slightly out of reach. In each case, there are likely to be differences regarding the categories above, for example the person throwing a punch is likely to carry out a quicker, heavier movement than the person reaching for the glass of water. Laban combines these four categories to create eight Efforts, as shown in Table 5.2.

In Laban's analysis, *space* or *focus* is either direct or indirect. Direct focus expresses that the person has a specific, singular intention or point of interest, whereas a movement characterised by indirect focus would have several points of interest. *Time* relates to the speed of the movement and the perception of how much time there is to perform the action. For example, five minutes could cause a person to feel under pressure and to move quickly, or the perception could be that five minutes is a lot of time to perform the given task, and the movement can therefore be performed in a sustained manner. *Weight* refers to the intensity of the force exerted during the movement, which can be either light or heavy. *Flow* describes the overall progression of the movement. The flow might be free, characterised by a lack of control and a high degree of fluidity, or bound, controlled and contained. Analysis of movement in this way has helped dancers and actors to embody different ways of physical

TABLE 5.2 Laban's Efforts

Effort	Space/Focus	Time	Weight	Flow
Punching	Direct	Quick	Heavy	Bound
Dabbing	Direct	Quick	Light	Bound
Pressing	Direct	Sustained	Heavy	Bound
Gliding	Direct	Sustained	Light	Free
Slashing	Indirect	Quick	Heavy	Free
Flicking	Indirect	Quick	Light	Free
Wringing	Indirect	Sustained	Heavy	Bound
Floating	Indirect	Sustained	Light	Free

expression and to move with inner intention. But what does this mean for teachers?

By the very nature of movement, it is difficult to articulate in words the different efforts described in Table 5.2. Laban's work gives us vocabulary to describe our movements, which in turn can help us to analyse and then adapt how we move to help us to communicate our intended message. There are many videos online showing how people, usually dancers and actors, interpret the eight Laban efforts. You could use these as a starting point and then consider how your own movements can be described in Laban's terms. For example: think about your movements in daily life. Which Effort(s) tends to describe how you move? Do you tend to move quickly, in a very focused and bound way, or are your movements freer, with no discernible focus or point of interest? We discussed above the importance of intentionality. By raising your awareness of how you tend to move, you will be able to be more intentional and use your physical movements to help communicate your message.

PAUSE FOR REFLECTION:

Now consider how Laban's Efforts might be incorporated into your teaching practice. Which Efforts could be useful in helping to achieve particular teaching aims? For example, when facilitating group work, your aim might be to monitor students' progress without being too intrusive. In this case, you might adopt a floating motion in the background. Or perhaps you need to encourage a group of students to focus their attention on the task at hand. In this case, you might adopt a pressing movement in order to appear assertive and to exhibit high 'status' (see Chapter 6). When planning your sessions, try planning how you will use different movements, or Efforts in Laban's terms, to help achieve your various aims as a teacher.

Michael Chekhov's psychological gesture

One of Stanslavski's students was a Russian actor, director and teacher, Michael Chekhov, a nephew of the Russian playwright, Anton Chekhov. Chekhov questioned the focus on emotions in the training of actors as it is difficult to portray accurately particular emotions on demand. For example, if you are trying to portray someone who is happy, there could be a number of degrees of happiness, some of which might be inappropriate for the context. Is the person happy because she is going to her favourite restaurant? Is she happy because she has passed her exams and has secured a place at university? Has she just won a life-changing amount of money? Each of these scenarios would call for a different level of happiness if the actor is to portray a believable character. The happiness displayed by someone who had just won the lottery would be strange, inauthentic, if it were displayed by someone who was happy about going to her favourite restaurant. This is where Chekhov's psychological gesture is of use.

The psychological gesture is a physical manifestation of the character's essence and the character's objectives. For example, if an actor is playing an aspiring politician or world leader, she might ask herself what is at the heart of this character; what is her objective? She might decide that power is the character's main objective. How, then, can the actor connect this psychological objective with her physical body? She might do this by portraying dominance or self-assuredness in her body, perhaps by standing tall and proud with chest out and feet planted securely in position; or she might press down onto an imaginary table, showing physical strength and dominance. This is a common technique used by actors to help them to 'get into character' and to connect emotions with the physical body. But how might this be applied in a teaching context?

In Chapter 1, we discussed how drama-based learning and gestures can be used to help students learn (cf. *nobjects* study in Chapter 1). Similarly, Chekhov's psychological gesture can be used by teachers to achieve their objectives and to aid their communication with their students. A good starting point is to identify the variety of objectives you might have as a teacher. Some of the teacher's objectives might include:

- To stimulate discussion
- To call students to action (to move into pairs/groups; to come to the whiteboard, etc.)
- To gain students' attention
- To display authority

How might these objectives be connected to the body using a gesture – or a series of gestures? Lenard Petit, artistic director at the Michael Checkhov Acting Studio in New York, teaches five overarching gestures:

- Push: stepping forwards with both hands stretched out as if pushing an object
- Pull: stepping backwards with both hands moving towards the body as if pulling on a rope

- Throw: engaging the whole body in an imaginary throw of a ball
- Lift: bending down to the floor and using both hands to lift an imaginary object
- Crush: clasp both hands in front of the body as if crushing an object

Some of these gestures might seem of little relevance to the usual objectives of a teacher. For example, how often are you likely to use the 'lift' or 'throw' gestures? The others, however, might be of use. For example, you might use a variation of the 'push' gesture when displaying authority and encouraging a student to stop talking. Or you might use a 'pull' gesture when trying to encourage a group of students to change direction in their discussions.

PAUSE FOR REFLECTION:

What are your different objectives when you are teaching? Think about how you usually achieve these objectives, such as getting students' attention, or stimulating discussion. To what extent do you use your body and gestures to help achieve these objectives? Try listing each of your objectives and think about how you could apply a psychological gesture to accompany each objective.

IN SUMMARY

Much of what we have discussed here is about raising our awareness of our body and movements and how we can use our physicality to help (or hinder) our teaching – and in turn help or hinder our students' learning. In many of the techniques from performance, and in several of the interviews in this book, a key factor when thinking about the body is intentionality: moving with an aim in mind and planning where you might position yourself at any given time. Some of the techniques discussed in this chapter might resonate with you; others might not. The aim here has been to raise awareness of your body and to provide some stimulus to consider your physical, intentional 'performance' as a teacher. However, not all performances are planned or intentional. Similarly, in the teaching context, not all aspects of a lesson are planned; some degree of spontaneity is involved when facilitating students' learning. This leads us on to the next aspect of performance which might be used as inspiration for developing our teaching practice: improvisation.

REFERENCES AND FURTHER READING

Barton, R. & Dal Vera, R. (2017) *Voice onstage and off*, 3rd ed. New York: Routledge.

Barton, R. & Sellers-Young, B. (2017) *Movement onstage and off*. New York: Routledge.

Chekhov, M. (1953/2002) *To the actor*. London: Routledge.

Ewan, V. & Sagovsky, K. (2016) *Laban's efforts in action: A movement handbook for actors*. London: Methuen.

Jay, D. (2018) No drama? Two theatrical strategies for initial teacher training. IATEFL Brighton Conference Selections, 228–229.

Lecoq, J. (2000) *The moving body*. London: Methuen.

McEvenue, K. (2001) *The Alexander technique for actors*. London: Methuen.

Mehrabian, A. (1981) *Silent messages: Implicit communication of emotions and attitudes*. Belmont, CA: Wadsworth.

Petit, L. (2010) *The Michael Checkhov handbook for the actor*. London: Routledge.

Snow, J. (2012) *Movement training for actors*. London: Methuen.

Chapter 6

Improvisation
Preparing for the unprepared

> "I think teachers and performers have a plan, but the best teachers and performers are able to adapt that plan and react to whatever happens in the room. And the process of planning and preparing is useful, a bit like training a muscle, but then it doesn't matter if you go completely off plan. The fact that you've prepared gives you the confidence to then teach or perform in the moment and to react to events as they unfold."
> **James Marples, Interview 7**

In Chapter 1, we explored some of the common anxieties we might have about teaching. Two of these were about not knowing the answers to students' questions and feeling ill-prepared when dealing with unexpected questions or events that arise in the classroom. In both of these cases, there is a concern about 'going off script' and not knowing what to do when put on the spot. Here, skills of improvisation might have something to offer.

WHAT IS IMPROVISATION?

To 'improvise' is derived from the Latin *improviso,* meaning unforeseen and not previously prepared. As a form of theatre, improvisation is a type of live performance which is unscripted; everything is made up on the spot, often with input from the audience. However, improvisation is not only a type of theatrical performance. The skills of improvisation are used more and more in learning and teaching contexts and in the professional development training of people working in a variety of sectors, including the use of 'applied improvisation' in non-performance settings such as business, marketing, and healthcare education (Tint & Froerer 2014).

Improvisation is often referred to as 'improv' or 'impro'. Impro originates from the theatre context whereas improv has its origins in comedic performance. The distinction between the two is also seemingly geographical, with improv used more in the North American context and impro in the British context. Having said this, some improvisation practitioners may disagree with this distinction. For our purposes, however, the precise usage of each term is not of great importance. An important player to mention here, particularly with regards to *impro,* is the British/Canadian actor and director, Keith Johnstone, whose books *Impro: Improvisation and the Theatre* (1987) and *Impro for Storytellers: Theatresports and the Art of Making Things Happen* (1999) discuss the art of improvisation, including the notion of 'status', which we discuss below. As the second book suggests, Keith Johnstone also introduced the concept of 'theatresports', which is a form of improvisational performance using a competition format in which teams 'compete' for points by showcasing their skills in improvisational comedy.

> Whether lecturing or tutoring you have to be prepared for questions that have to be answered with speed, wit and knowledge. The improvisation aspect is not unlike Theatresports.
>
> Susan Maloney, Interview 5

IMPROVISATION IN TEACHING

> As a practical point for training teachers, one of the basic concepts in improv is 'yes, and...'.
>
> Martin Billingham, Interview 6

So what has this got to do with teaching? In a biography of Keith Johnstone, Theresa Dudeck (2013: 1) points out that "for him (Johnstone), theatre is an informal classroom where life experiences can be fleshed out collaboratively in order to re-create ... imaginative stories spontaneously". So in his original concept of impro(visation), Johnstone alluded clearly to the educational and pedagogic value of this form of theatre.

Here, we can also refer back to Table 1.1. Some of the anxieties frequently cited by teachers, particularly by those relatively new to teaching, relate to the fear of being put on the spot and dealing with the unexpected. As we have seen above, improvisation is all about thinking and acting on the spot; thinking and acting in the moment, so skills of improvisation are worth considering as teachers.

There is also much research showing that more experienced and more effective teachers use improvisation more than novice teachers, whilst also having a greater repertoire of 'scripts' or structures for their teaching (e.g. Sawyer 2011). This does not mean we simply 'make it up as we go along'. Sawyer (2011: 2) refers to this as "disciplined improvisation", highlighting that effective teachers operate within a broad plan and structure whilst maintaining the freedom to improvise and 'go off script'.

Another type of performance in which prepared material and improvised material is delivered is stand-up comedy. Stand-up comedian and educator, Martin Billingham (Interview 6) has written about the potential ways in which teachers might learn from the stand-up comedian's craft (Billingham 2020). A comedian co-constructs and adapts the performance in collaboration with the audience. The existence of a plan in stand-up comedy is perhaps closer to the teaching context, whereas improv performance does not include pre-prepared materials. With specific reference to teaching, Martin Billingham highlights the importance of knowing when to depart from the planned material:

> "The big thing about people at the beginning of their teaching experience is that they often cling on to their lesson plan."
>
> (Martin Billingham, Interview 6)

This feeling that everything must go according to plan – and that there is only one possible plan – stifles dynamism and creativity, and can exacerbate anxiety in the form of *must*-statements, as discussed in Chapter 3, for example I *must* get through everything on my plan; I *must* teach this part of the session in the way it has been planned. In a sense, then, skills of improvisation can free us from adhering to such a rigid plan, and help us to negotiate the learning and teaching encounter in partnership with our students. Some of the benefits to teachers of developing skills of improvisation are:

- Improved skills of interaction
- Improved clarity, creativity, and spontaneity
- Increased awareness of self
- An increased sense of presence – thinking and acting in the moment
- Improved confidence and self-efficacy
- Increased confidence to respond to unexpected questions and situations

(Adapted from Toivanen et al. 2011)

There are many 'rules' of improvisation that have been proposed by various theatre teachers over the years. As Martin Billingham tells us, "one of the basic concepts in improv is 'yes, and...'" (Interview 6). This helps to keep the flow of thoughts and ideas moving and creates an environment where all ideas are accepted. When researching improvisational theatre, another name in particular arises frequently: the late American actor, writer, and teacher, Del Close, who co-founded the ImprovOlympic Theater (now known as the iO Theater) in Chicago with his partner, Charna Halpern. Del Close devised a set of 'Eleven Commandments' in improv:

1. You are all supporting actors.
2. Always check your impulses.
3. Never enter a scene unless you are needed.
4. Save your fellow actor, don't worry about the piece.
5. Your prime responsibility is to support.
6. Work at the top of your brains at all times.
7. Never underestimate or condescend to your audience.
8. No jokes (unless it is tipped in front that it is a joke).
9. Trust your fellow actors to support you; trust them to come through if you lay something heavy on them; trust yourself.
10. Avoid judging what is going down except in terms of whether it needs help (either by entering or cutting), what can best follow, or how you can support it imaginatively if your support is called for.
11. Listen.

PAUSE FOR REFLECTION:

In what ways can you relate these rules of improvisation to your teaching context? Think about how you respond to unplanned scenarios in the classroom. Are you impulsive? Do you enter into discussions between students 'uninvited'? In what ways do you support the action that takes place in the classroom? In what ways do you lead it? To what extent are your students co-actors – co-designers – during the lesson?

One point to highlight here is Del Close's first 'commandment' – you are all supporting actors. We can apply this to the teaching context by considering our students to be co-designers and co-editors of the lesson. Martin Billingham makes this point in relation to stand-up comedy: "the thing with stand-up comedy is you are writing and editing the show with the audience" (Interview 6). In a teaching context, this helps to shift the focus from teacher to student. A similar comment can be made about commandment 5: your prime responsibility is to support. Finally, I would highlight (active) listening from Del Close's list. This is linked to number 2 – check your impulses. An important part of our teaching 'performance' is what happens when we are *not* speaking, moving, or actively doing something. We are able to respond in the moment with greater impact if we listen carefully to what others are saying – in this case, our students.

The key message for us as teachers is that we should learn not to fear the unexpected, but to view teaching and learning as a semi-structured experience which can, and will, develop according to ongoing dialogue and negotiation with our students. Active listening, collaboration, and mutual respect are at the heart of improvisation, and these are all qualities which also contribute to good teaching, highlighting that an ability to improvise will also help to foster creativity, collaboration, critical thinking, and communication in our students.

The other reason for considering improvisation in the teaching context is because the very essence of improvisation is remarkably aligned with current notions of how we can teach most effectively, namely through active learning. We explore this more in Chapter 7, but a quote here from Berk and Trieber (2009) will help to explain at this point why improvisation is an important skill – for teachers and students – in any classroom where active learning is taking place.

> Traditional theatre uses a script to guide everything, from the sets, props, and costumes to the choice of actors for the various roles. The director controls the entire production with no input from the audience ... In contrast, improvisational theatre has no script ... the audience participates by deciding the topic or story line. When improvisation is reformatted into small-group collaborative learning activities in a learner-centred environment, it can be a powerful teaching tool.
>
> (Berk & Trieber 2009: 30)

As Berk and Trieber explain, improvisation involves *collaboration*. Teaching is no longer about the teacher – or certainly not just about the teacher – but instead the students are an integral part of the action.

105

Sofia Alexiadou (Interview 1) likens this to immersive theatre, where audiences no longer sit passively watching a performance, but instead are actively involved in formulating and shaping the performance.

> "We are discussing more and more about immersive theatre, so I mean when I was studying it was sort of a performance with the lecturer – it was a one-way thing; he was just feeding us. But now I think it's more like immersive theatre."
>
> (Sofia Alexiadou, Interview 1)

So improvisation, as well as helping teachers to hone useful skills, encourages us to shift the focus onto our students so that we share the teaching and learning space in a more collaborative, interactive, and immersive way.

STATUS

We have already mentioned the term 'status' above, which is a key concept in improvisation. In theatre terms, status is about distance between characters, particularly regarding power relations between characters. In Keith Johnstone's conceptualisation of status (Johnstone (1987), there is a clear focus on action, that is, what a character *does* rather than the status a person has because of their place in society. This means actors can play with status by portraying a character differently to how the audience might expect. For example, a king would have high social status, but an actor might play with the audience's expectations by portraying the character with low status: as weak, unconfident, and deferential, for example.

PAUSE FOR REFLECTION:

How does Keith Johnstone's concept of status relate to teaching? Reflect on your own status when you are teaching; how do you portray yourself? What is the 'power' distance between you and your students? Are you quite authoritarian? Are you very approachable? Does your status change? If so, depending on what? Do you 'play' a particular status consciously? Or is it an inherent part of your teacher persona and style?

Answers to these questions might help you to become more aware of how you portray yourself as a teacher, and how your students might perceive you in status terms. This heightened self-awareness also means that you will be able to play with different statuses and (re)act in the moment: that is to say – improvise. Martin Billingham puts this very well in the context of hecklers and stand-up comedy:

> "The worst thing you can do with a heckler is to absolutely squish them, because really it's an invitation to play, to be involved. The best thing to do is to match the level of the heckler ... The worst thing to do is to either totally ignore it or to be too heavy handed. You want to treat it as if it's an invitation to play, but you are in control of that play. Both the stand-up comedian and the teacher are in constant negotiation with their audience, or students, as to what happens."
>
> (Martin Billingham, Interview 6)

Martin Billingham makes a useful point about negotiation as a shared aspect between teaching and stand-up comedy. If we, as teachers, are able to adapt our reactions and persona, or status, to the situations and discussions that arise in class, we are better equipped to respond effectively and appropriately in the moment, whether this be a response to an unexpected question, a response to a student's (mis)behaviour, or otherwise.

PLAYING WITH STATUS AS A TEACHER

Keith Johnstone also made explicit links between his concept of status in improvisational theatre and in the teaching context. He reflected on different types of teachers that he had encountered, some of which might be familiar to you:

1   The teacher who is likeable, and who is largely well liked by students, but who is unable to keep discipline and order.
2   The teacher who is disliked, even feared by students. There is rarely a need for the teacher to keep discipline because students are too scared to misbehave.
3   The teacher who is well liked by students. Like Teacher 2, this teacher rarely needs to keep discipline. She is very human, jokes with students, but can use her persona and stillness to get students' attention.

(Johnstone 1987: 35)

107

Johnstone concluded that Teacher 1 exhibited low status; unable to react or respond as events in the classroom unfolded. Teacher 1 is like an imposter and never seems to command the teaching space. Teacher 2, on the other hand, exhibited constant high status behaviour. Like Teacher 1, Teacher 2 also does not react to events as they develop; however, the difference is that the high status means Teacher 2 is in 'control'. Teacher 3 is able to play with status; to improvise to suit the developing needs of the class, raising or lowering her status in response to students' behaviour and responses.

Johnstone proposes several techniques for playing with status. These were devised primarily for actors in the context of theatre, but some are applicable to teaching. Three in particular are worth mentioning:

- **Placing and length of gap fillers**
  When you are speaking and you come to a point where you need to think, you might make some kind of noise or utterance which indicates that you are processing your thoughts and deciding what to say next (much like the vocal nonverbals discussed in Chapter 4). A common way of doing this is to say 'err...' or 'umm...'. Keith Johnstone makes several points about how these little gap fillers can raise or lower our status. A weak gap filler at the beginning of a sentence can give the impression that the teacher is unsure or hesitant. By moving the gap filler to the middle of a sentence, this can give the impression of higher status, and thus the perception of strength and confidence. However, by moving the gap filler back to the beginning of the sentence, but making it longer and more emphatic, status is raised further.
- **Eye contact**
  Though disputed, it is believed that holding eye contact gives the impression of higher status, power, and confidence. In a teaching context, Keith Johnstone explains that breaking eye contact can also be a high status move as long as you do not re-establish eye contact shortly after looking away.
- **Head movement**
  The final technique to mention here is movement of the head, or rather keeping it still. Johnstone cites this as one of the most simple and effective ways of raising your status. Keeping the head still while speaking lends the speaker an air of calm authority, which, according to Johnstone, is perceived by

students as authoritative but poised, much like Teacher 3 in Johnstone's different types of teacher status above.

Outside of acting and improvisation circles, the concept of status is rather unfamiliar, but Johnstone claims many teachers have applied some of his techniques to great effect in the classroom. Johnstone's work on status is about connecting with others' behaviours and responding in the moment to those behaviours. This seems to be a useful skill for teachers to explore. One caveat here is that actors hone these skills in training and rehearsals before they perform in front of an audience. As teachers, we rarely have the luxury of rehearsals, so experimentation with raising and lowering status, and identifying our preferred status, can be done in everyday life situations instead. You can try out the techniques above, for example, when talking to friends or colleagues, and see what happens. If you notice any positive effects, you could then try these out in class. Having said this, one type of 'rehearsal' space for teachers could be microteaching (see Chapter 2), so you could use a microteaching session to focus explicitly on experimenting with status.

> Also I think the use of humour and status is important. So for example, students might be playing on their phones, and it's about how you manage that. And you can do that with humour in a way that doesn't make people feel small or stupid but it clearly outlines what you expect. This ties into notions of etiquette in the theatre or classroom. I saw a performance of The Nico Project with Maxine Peake, and a man, at quite an intense moment, got up to go to the toilet. You really felt sorry for him because it was embarrassing for him. And the actress, Peake, acknowledged it. It just so happened that the line was about leaving, so she just looked at the man and raised an eyebrow. So it's about knowing when you can disrupt your script to acknowledge what's going on in the room.
>
> Clare Chandler, Interview 10

WHAT WOULD I DO IF...?

Earlier in Chapters 3 and 5, we discussed how some of the ideas of the famous Russian actor and director, Konstantin Stanislavski, might be applied to teaching. Chapter 5, in particular, explored how concepts such as re-education and motivation can be used when thinking about how we use our bodies and physical gestures as teachers. Another useful concept from Stanislavski is the 'magic if'. In Stanislavski's System, the 'magic if' is a tool used by actors to open up their imagination in order to find out more, in an imaginary but realistic sense, about their characters. It involves asking a series of 'what if' questions in order to take the imagination to a set of fictional, but possible, circumstances. From this definition, the link to improvisation becomes quite apparent: the actor is deciding on the questions (the 'what if' questions) and is also formulating the answers. Stanislavski used this tool in order to enable his actors to hone their ability to imagine fictitious, but realistic circumstances.

Here is an example of a magic if exercise from Nick O'Brien, director of The Stanislavski Experience, which provides workshops and acting coaching, focusing in particular on the work and ideas of Stanislavski. The example here is specifically for actors, but we will explore how this might be adapted for us as teachers:

1   Imagine you are in class and time has moved on 12 hours from the actual time on the clock right now. Ask yourself questions like: What if I had already been in this class for 12 hours? How would I feel right now?

2   Imagine these new circumstances using the magic if. What if I was still in this class 12 hours from now? How would the classroom look? What would my family be thinking? Would they be worried? How would I get home?

3   Improvise in your mind how you would respond in these new circumstances. What if I got up and told the teacher I had to leave? What if I started to fall asleep? What if I couldn't find my phone to call home?

4   Allow your imagination to lead and let imagined actions flow out of your responses to the 'what if' questions. Try not to force your responses and reactions.

(Adapted from O'Brien 2018: 4)

Exercise: the teacher's magic if

Now let's transfer the example above to our context of teaching in universities. As a starting point for asking 'what if' questions, we can take the common anxiety about unexpected questions from students (see Table 1.1).

1   Context: you have 10 students in a tutorial group. In the session last week, one of your students asked a question that was relevant to the topic of discussion, but you simply didn't know

the answer – and it was a question to which you think you should have known the answer. In that situation, you became embarrassed and started trying to respond to the question. You were stuttering, hesitating, and you think it was obvious to the students that you were not prepared for that question.

2 Now imagine time has moved on a full week and you are with that same tutorial group once again. Imagine how you are feeling now. What if that student asks me another difficult question? What if I get the feeling she/he is challenging me on purpose?

3 Imagine feeling completely different to how you felt last week. Imagine now feeling confident, with raised status. What if I tell the student I don't know the answer? What if I ask the student to research possible answers to the question for next week? What if I ask the rest of the class to discuss the question? What if I shift attention from myself and focus instead on the other actors – the students – so that we negotiate how this scenario develops?

This exercise gives you an opportunity to think through, in a realistic way, based on (potentially) real events, how you might respond in a given set of circumstances. To repeat Sawyer's words at the beginning of this chapter, it allows us to engage in "disciplined improvisation" (Sawyer 2011: 2). We have in our toolkit a set of potential questions, answers, scripts, and scenarios, none of which may ever materialise exactly as we have imagined, but we are able to improvise and respond in the moment because we can draw on our well trained imagination with its constantly questioning 'what if' scenarios. You might also notice that this kind of thinking can help us to reframe some of the imagined scenarios. As we discussed in Chapter 3, we can exacerbate our own anxieties by indulging in what Berry and Edelstein (2009) call *awfulizing* (see Table 3.2). In step 2 in the exercise above, the 'what if' questions are following negative, awfulizing thought processes. By working through a situation like this, using the magic if, you can reframe the 'what if' questions so that you think of more practical, positive solutions, as in step 3 above.

> Answering unexpected questions (that really can come out of nowhere, can test the edges of my knowledge, and sometimes seem to be tied to the present topic in only the most tenuous ways) really requires that same 'Yes, and' attitude that an improv actor has.

> Sometimes being willing to be wrong (which is how teachers feel about saying "I don't know") and willing to say "That's a good question. I'm going to find out." or "Let's look that up!" is what is needed and is part of the ability to take risks that improv hones.
>
> Megan Bylsma, Interview 8

THE MEISNER TECHNIQUE

Sanford Meisner was an American actor and acting teacher who became famous for developing the Meisner technique (Meisner & Longwell 1987). Meisner's work is of interest in relation to improvisation because he focused on developing actors' abilities to get out of their heads and to respond spontaneously to a given situation that arises. Meisner was interested in developing actors' listening skills – as opposed to acting in response to scripted, rehearsed dialogue – and he wanted actors to react instinctively, in the moment, to what they had listened to. In this way, Meisner was a strong proponent of improvisation and learning to react to others' impulses.

The most famous aspect of the Meisner technique is the repetition exercise. The aim is to practise repeating statements (not questions) in response to changes in the other person's (actor's) behaviour or appearance. Person A makes a statement in relation to person B. Person B repeats the statement. The repetitions continue until one person notices a change and responds by changing the statement. For example:

A: You have long hair.
B: I have long hair.
A: You have long hair.
B: I have long hair
A: You are smiling.
B: I am smiling.
A: You stopped smiling.
B: I stopped smiling.

In this example, person A starts by commenting on person B's hair. At some point, presumably because the situation feels strange or absurd, person B starts to smile. Person A notices this change and responds by saying: 'You are smiling'. When there is another change in behaviour or appearance, this is reflected again in person A's new statement: 'You stopped smiling'. The aim here is to learn to trust your instincts and observations, and to react to these observations impulsively. This exercise also trains the actors' listening skills, as they have to repeat what is said by their partner in a spontaneous way.

So what has this got to do with teaching? Clearly, we are not likely to sit opposite one of our students and play this repetition game. However, the skills that are learned from this technique are directly applicable to many aspects of life, teaching included. We can think about this in relation to the scenario in the exercise on the magic if above, where the teacher is concerned about not knowing the answer to a student's question.

PAUSE FOR REFLECTION:

Imagine the scenario again in which one of your students asks you a question to which you do not know the answer. How might the Meisner repetition exercise help you to improvise at this moment? Remember this technique encourages you to:

- Observe others
- Identify behaviours displayed by others
- Say what you see
- Respond in the moment

The first point here is that you shift attention on to the student who asked the question. Using your skills of observation, you are better able to identify the behaviour – the intent – behind the student's question. You are unlikely to follow the Meisner technique fully by repeating what the student says; however, you can respond in the moment depending on the intent you have observed behind the student's question. For example, if you have the impression that the student wants to challenge your knowledge in front of the other students, you can use this observation as a pretext to push the question back to the student, similar to the ping-pong exchange in the Meisner repetition exercise. You could say, for example: 'You are asking an interesting question.' Or 'Your question is great in the context of ..., which we will explore next semester.' You are responding to the student's *behaviour* or *intent* rather than responding to the challenge to your knowledge and authority, perceived or real. Similarly, with better skills of observation and an ability to react to others' behaviours, you will also be able to identify more easily whether the student's question simply comes from a place of genuine curiosity.

IMPROVISATION TECHNIQUES FOR YOU AND YOUR STUDENTS

So far, we have discussed improvisation as a performative aspect of the teacher's role. However, there is also a growing body of literature about the use of improvisation to help students learn (e.g. Berk & Trieber 2009; Diamond & Christensen 2005; Hoffman-Longtin et al. 2018). The influential American academic, educator, and actress, Viola Spolin, created around 200 improvisation games, which have been important in the training of many actors (Spolin 1999). Several of these games are also applicable in teaching contexts, some of which I have used in my own teaching with postgraduate researchers who are at the beginning of their teaching experience. Here is a brief introduction to three of these. Think about how you might use similar activities in your own teaching context.

Exercise 1: one word at a time

Students sit in a circle and think of a title for a story, for example A Memorable Day. Go round the circle with each person using one word to tell the story. The story must make sense. Keep going round the circle with each person building the story one word at a time until the narrative no longer makes sense. For example:

A: I
B: once
C: flew
D: to
A: Paris
B: on
C: holiday
D: which
A: is
B: where
C: I
D: met
A: my
B: fiancée

The example here is obviously a generic story. However, you can use this improv game in your subject context. Berk and Trieber (2009) explain how they used this technique to help students review subject content in a Mental Health and Stress Management course. They asked students to write down keywords on the subject of wellness and mental health. This activity allowed students to activate their thinking around the subject before being asked to improvise. The game then followed the same process as in my example above, with each student telling a story (reviewing subject content) one word at a time (Berk & Trieber 2009: 40–43).

PAUSE FOR REFLECTION:

Consider how you could use this improvisation game in your own teaching context.

- Think of a subject/module you teach.
- What are the keywords and concepts in that subject?
- Think about how you could use a one-word-at-a-time activity to help students review key content before an assessment; as a warm-up activity to ascertain existing knowledge at the beginning of a class/series of classes; to review learning as an informal, formative assessment in a plenary at the end of a class...

Exercise 2: last word response

A slightly more difficult variation of the one-word-at-a-time activity is 'last word response'. This exercise helps us to listen carefully and to think ahead during a conversation. This skill is very useful when teaching and responding to unknown or unexpected questions.

The exercise starts with one person making a statement. The next person must begin their response using the last word in the previous person's statement. For example:

A: I really need to study more <u>often</u>.
B: <u>Often</u> I think about doing just <u>that</u>.
A: <u>That</u> is the problem; I'm just too <u>busy</u>.
B: <u>Busy</u> people always say that, but you have to make <u>time</u>.
A: <u>Time</u> is something I just don't have!

As the focus here is on connecting sentences using the last word in the preceding sentence, players are faced with the added difficulty of beginning their response with the last word, whilst also creating a coherent story using the subject content and keywords under review. This variation might therefore be used when students (and you!) have had some practice at improvising.

Exercise 3: speech tag

In Viola Spolin's long list of improvisation games, speech tag was often used when training actors as a follow-on from the one-word-at-a-time activity. In speech tag, a group of students tells a collaborative story about a subject that has been studied recently in class; however, this time, players are not limited to one word. One student begins and then another student can tag the speaker on the shoulder when she/he would like to take over. Here is an example from my own disciplinary context of languages, namely German:

Student 1: There are four cases in German: the nominative, the accusative, the dative, and the genitive. These can be difficult for English speakers to learn because we do not have a case system in English- (Student 2 tags Student 1).

Student 2: Yes, and the cases mean that word order in German can be more flexible than in English because you can easily identify the subject, direct and indirect object of a sentence because of the case endings- (Student 3 tags Student 2).

Student 3: Yes, and the endings are also determined by the gender of nouns. There are three genders in German: masculine, feminine, and neuter, and these genders have specific endings in different cases- (Student 2 tags Student 3).

Student 2: Yes, and for example...

Notice that each student begins with the golden rule: 'yes, and...'. At the end of the activity, the group can spend some time debriefing and reviewing the story and the responses that were given. How accurate was the information presented? Why did each player decide to take over at each point? Was it because they thought there was a mistake in the previous student's speech, or did they just have something interesting to add? Consider how you might adapt this activity to your own subject context.

IN SUMMARY

Due to the collaborative and often spontaneous nature of teaching, I would argue that teaching itself is an *improvisational* act. This view is well aligned with current teaching philosophies which encourage dynamic and collaborative practices between teachers and students. In this chapter, we have seen just a few improvisation techniques that could be used by teachers both to enhance performance in the teacher role, and also to facilitate students' learning. As we discussed at the beginning of this chapter, improvisation in a theatre context is about audience participation and co-creation of a theatrical piece by performers and spectators. In essence, improvisation has properties of inclusivity and interactivity, both of which are key topics in learning and teaching in contemporary higher education. Active learning and inclusion, as they relate to performance, are the topic of our final chapter.

 REFERENCES AND FURTHER READING

Berk, R. A. & Trieber, R. H. (2009) Whose classroom is it, anyway? Improvisation as a teaching tool. *Journal on Excellence in College Teaching* 20(3), 29–60.

Berry, M. & Edelstein, M. R. (2009) *Stage fright. 40 Stars tell you how they beat America's #1 fear.* Tucson: See Sharp Press.

Billingham, M. (2020) 'Ah Ha! And Ha Ha!' Teaching and stand-up comedy. *NATE: Teaching English* 22.

Diamond, M. R. & Christensen, M. H. (2005) Bravo! Do acting games promote learning in the college classroom? *Journal on Excellence in College Teaching* 16(2), 55–67.

Dudeck, T. R. (2013) *Keith Johnstone. A Critical Biography.* London: Bloomsbury.

Esper, W. & DiMarco, D. (2008) *The actor's art and craft. William Esper teaches the Meisner technique.* New York: Anchor.

Halpern, C., Close, D., & Johnson, K. (1994) *Truth in comedy: The manual of improvisation.* Colorado Springs: Meriwether.

Hoffmann-Longtin, K., Rossing, J. P., & Weinstein, E. (2018) Twelve tips for using applied improvisation in medical education. *Medical Teacher* 40(4), 351–356.

Johnstone, K. (1987) *Impro: Improvisation and the theatre.* Oxford: Routledge.

Johnstone, K. (1999) *Impro for storytellers: Theatresports and the art of making things happen*. Oxford: Routledge.

Meisner, S., & Longwell, D. (1987) *Sanford Meisner on acting*. New York: Vintage.

O'Brien, N. (2018) *Stanislavski in practice. Exercises for students*, 2nd ed. Oxford: Routledge.

Sawyer, R. K. (2011) What makes good teachers great? The artful balance of structure and improvisation. In: R. K. Sawyer (ed) *Structure and improvisation in creative teaching*. Cambridge: CUP.

Spolin, V. (1986) *Theatre games for the classroom: A teacher's handbook*. Evanston: Northwestern University Press.

Spolin, V. (1999) *Improvisation for the theatre: A handbook of teaching and directing techniques*, 3rd ed. Evanston: Northwestern University Press.

Tint, B. & Froerer, A. (2014) Delphi study summary. Applied improvisation network. Available at: https://tinyurl.com/y48e2ezd (accessed 7 June 2019).

Toivanen, T., Komulainen, K., & Ruismäki, H. (2011) Drama education and improvisation as a resource of teacher student's creativity. *Procedia Social and Behavioral Sciences* 12, 60–69.

Chapter 7

Performance, active learning, and inclusivity

> "I think if you possess performing arts skills you already have strategies to draw upon to engage others, to react to surprises and to think on your feet ... When you dance or perform with others, mutual trust is vital ... Underpinning this is the creation of trust amongst students and peers. If you have trust, there is more willingness to be vulnerable, to take risks and to take ownership of the outcomes."
>
> **Susan Maloney, Interview 5**

In Chapter 1, I highlighted a potential conflict that arises from focusing on the teacher (and the teacher's performance) at a time when there is increasingly strong evidence that our students learn more effectively when we shift our attention from teacher to student by using learner-centred methods. However, I do not see these two endeavours – improving the teacher's performance and placing learners at the centre of the learning experience – as mutually exclusive. In fact, I would argue that teaching in a classroom where active learning is taking place, requires far more skill, and performance technique, than a situation where a teacher delivers a didactic transmission of knowledge in a lecture format.

This final chapter explores what we mean by active learning, and invites you to reflect on how some of the performance aspects discussed earlier might help you to create a more learner-centred, engaging environment. We also highlight the important issue of inclusivity in our teaching practice, and consider how the teacher's enhanced performance can help to make teaching more inclusive.

WHAT IS ACTIVE LEARNING?

The concept of active learning is in some ways self-explanatory: the idea that students learn by actively engaging with material, with other students, and with the teacher(s) in order to construct their own knowledge. However, active learning can take many forms, or rather, many different approaches can be classed as active learning. I started this chapter by mentioning the term 'learner-centred'. In essence, there are several terms which are often used to describe largely the same concept: learner-centred, student-centred, and active learning. At the heart of this concept is the focus on *learning* (and hence the learner) as opposed to *teaching* (and hence the teacher). The teacher then becomes a facilitator of learning rather than a disseminator of knowledge.

PAUSE FOR REFLECTION:

How do you define active learning? What kinds of activities do you use frequently in order to engage your students? How does your role, your performance, differ when you are leading an active learning session compared with when you are delivering a lecture?

Active learning is rooted in constructivism, a theory that views learning as a meaning-making process, in which learners construct knowledge on the basis of their existing understanding and experiences. Building on this, Lev Vygotsky (1978) emphasised the importance of social interaction in learning, taking a social constructivist view of learning, in which students construct their learning through interaction with others. Inherent in this theoretical standpoint is the idea of *activity*.

Despite the prevalence of didactic lectures in many universities, the idea of active learning is not new. Specifically in the higher education context, Chickering and Gamson explained the concept in the 1980s in their '*Seven Principles for Good Practice in Undergraduate Education*':

> Learning is not a spectator sport. Students do not learn much just by sitting in classes listening to teachers, memorizing pre-packaged assignments, and spitting out answers. They must talk about what they are learning, write about it, relate it to past experiences, apply it to their daily lives. They must make what they learn part of themselves.
>
> (Chickering & Gamson 1987: 4)

Despite early acknowledgments such as this from Chickering and Gamson, active learning methods have only relatively recently started to receive greater attention in higher education, as opposed to primary and secondary education, where purely didactic, teacher-centred instruction is less prevalent. This difference in uptake is reflected in the literature, where most research on active learning has been conducted in the context of school teaching. One notable exception is Maryellen Weimar's *Learner-Centered Teaching,* originally published in first edition in 2002. Weimar (2013) starts with the contention that most teaching in universities is teacher-centred, and offers examples of how to shift to more student-centred approaches. More recently, interest in active learning in higher education has grown considerably, as have efforts to provide evidence for the effectiveness of using active learning methods in university teaching (e.g. Freeman et al. 2014; Roberts 2019; Wieman 2014). Indeed, a journal dedicated solely to this topic has been in existence since 2000: *Active Learning in Higher Education* – and evidence from much of the work that has been carried out in recent years is now starting to translate into teaching practice.

ACTIVE LEARNING AND PEDAGOGY OF THE OPPRESSED

We have focused throughout this book on the various performative aspects of the teacher's role, but we have also seen that collaboration and co-production are at the heart of many types of performance. In classrooms where active learning is taking place, we can extend this ethos of collaboration to the teaching and learning context, where the teacher is no longer the sole, focal 'performer', but is instead surrounded by 'co-performers' – the students who play active roles in their learning rather than passively receiving wisdom from the 'sage on the stage'. Sofia Alexiadou, in Interview 1, captured very well the link between performance and active learning, where she drew the comparison between immersive theatre and students who are actively engaged in the classroom.

Active engagement in collaborative learning is evocative of Brazilian educator, Paulo Freire's *Pedagogy of the Oppressed.* In this influential book, published in Portuguese in 1968 and translated into English in 1970, Freire uses the concept of banking as a metaphor to describe traditional, didactic teaching, in which students are empty deposit boxes that are filled with knowledge by teachers. Freire explains: "in the banking concept of education, knowledge is a gift bestowed by those who consider themselves knowledgeable upon those whom they consider to know nothing"

(Freire 1970: 72). Freire considers this to be an oppressive ideology which stifles students' critical thinking and places the teacher, rather than the student, at the centre of the educational process in the following ways:

a   "the teacher teaches and the students are taught;
b   the teacher knows everything and the students know nothing;
c   the teacher thinks and the students are thought about;
d   the teacher talks and the students listen – meekly;
e   the teacher disciplines and the students are disciplined;
f   the teacher chooses and enforces his choice, and the students comply;
g   the teacher acts and the students have the illusion of acting through the action of the teacher;
h   the teacher chooses the program content, and the students (who were not consulted) adapt to it;
i   the teacher confuses the authority of knowledge with his or her own professional authority, which she and he sets in opposition to the freedom of the students;
j   the teacher is the Subject of the learning process, while the pupils are mere Objects" (Freire 1970: 73).

The links between Freire's ideas and active learning are probably self-evident, that is, promoting a shift in emphasis away from the teacher, and teaching, and focusing instead on the learner, and learning. At this point, though, it is not clear how all this is relevant to our discussion of performance. The link here is Brazilian political activist and theatre practitioner, Augusto Boal's *Theatre of the Oppressed*, which was first published in 1973.

ACTIVE LEARNING AND THEATRE OF THE OPPRESSED

Augusto Boal was a friend of Paulo Freire and was heavily influenced by the ideas in Freire's *Pedagogy of the Oppressed*. Boal was also inspired by the famous German playwright, Berthold Brecht, whose *Lehrstücke* (translated by Brecht as 'teaching plays') focused on breaking down the divide between actors and audience, creating a *Verfremdungseffekt* (distancing or alienating effect) to prevent the audience from becoming too immersed in the narrative, and instead adopting a more active, conscious, critical role as spectator. Boal emphasised the need for interaction and dialogue between spectators and performers;

the need for audiences to be active in order to effect social and political change. If we explore theatre of the oppressed in Boal's own words, the similarities between this concept, or method, and Freire's pedagogy of the oppressed, become clear:

> The members of the audience must become the Character: possess him, take his place – not obey him, but guide him, show him the path they think right. In this way the Spectator becoming the Spect-Actor is dramatically opposed to the other members of the audience, free to invade the scene and appropriate the power of the actor ... I, Augusto Boal, want the Spectator to take on the role of Actor and invade the Character and the stage. I want him to occupy his own Space and offer solutions.
>
> (Boal 2000: xx–xxi)

The notion of empowerment and engagement of the audience members aligns with the idea that students should be actively engaged in their learning. The concept of Spect-Actors, who step into the actors' shoes and decide how the piece will progress, is reminiscent of an active learning classroom, where students do not sit like passive deposit boxes, in Freire's terms, but instead are co-creators of the learning that takes place. Boal devised techniques and games to empower his audiences to invade the scene and to contribute to the development of the action on stage. Some of the key techniques in Boal's methods are: Image Theatre, Forum Theatre, and Rainbow of Desire. Forum Theatre, in particular, is easy to adapt to a variety of teaching contexts so we will explore this in more detail below. Boal published his techniques and theatre games in 1992 as *Games for Actors and Non-actors* (Boal 2002), many of which can be adapted to teaching contexts to promote performative, active learning.

The Joker

One of the key roles described by Boal is the so-called Joker. For Boal, the Joker refers to the 'Joker' card in a deck of playing cards. The Joker is a versatile role but is rarely in the foreground as a protagonist. The Joker is a facilitator, a director, and a mediator. This role can be directly transferred to the teaching context, where a teacher, who is committed to engaging students in active learning, might assume the role of a facilitator rather than a didactic disseminator of knowledge.

Forum theatre

A particularly interesting feature of Boal's method is forum theatre. In this type of theatre, a piece is acted out, usually with a character experiencing some form of oppression. The spectators can shout 'Stop!' at any time and become part of the theatrical action, either by proposing an alternative solution to the oppressed character's problems or by stepping into the role of the protagonist and acting out her/his alternative course of action. This is where spectators become spect-actors, contributing to and shaping the story as it plays out on stage. This technique is referred to as forum theatre because the theatrical action becomes a topic for discussion about possible solutions to problems, much like a public forum, only in dramatic form.

Forum theatre can be used as an active learning activity. The focus on oppression in Boal's original concept can be changed so that students act out and discuss scenarios, problems, and topics related to the course of study. This can work very well for ethical discussions in a variety of disciplines, but also in practical demonstrations, such as in laboratory subjects. The 'rules' of the game of forum theatre are quite simple:

1   The students watch a performance (this could be adapted to a demonstration, a discussion, a dialogue, whatever is relevant to your teaching context).
2   At the end of this piece, students have some time to consider how they might change the sequence of events they have seen, and think of alternative solutions to the problems/issues/topics presented.
3   The piece is then repeated, but this time students may shout 'Stop!' at any time if they would like to propose an alternative sequence of events or an alternative solution. This is the point at which spectators become spect-actors.
4   The Joker acts as a facilitator and can support students who are nervous about proposing their alternative ideas.
5   The Joker should avoid making decisions or leading the discussion/action. Instead, the Joker can act as a mirror, posing questions to the group to stimulate further thought and discussion, for example: Does this solution work? How will it affect character X? Does this solution/course of action have any disadvantages?

PAUSE FOR REFLECTION:

Think about your own teaching context and your subject discipline. What are the key 'problems', discussion points, or practical elements in the courses that you teach? How do you usually stimulate discussion and activity surrounding these topics and issues? Consider how you might adapt your methods to incorporate a performative, forum theatre element so that your students become part of the action as spect-actors.

It might seem daunting at first to use theatrical techniques to enhance the activity and interactivity in the classroom. However, as Timpson and Burgoyne (2014) point out, it is not necessary to be an actor or a performer to take inspiration from techniques used in the theatre of the oppressed, or other dramatic methods. If we keep in mind our aim – to engage students actively in their learning – we can feel empowered to explore different ways of achieving this aim. A more conventional way of stimulating discussion, for example, might be to use case studies and to ask students to discuss each case and to evaluate the solutions proposed. Thinking in these terms, forum theatre does not seem particularly radical or daunting. We are simply adapting a text-based case study and asking students to be more physically active. After all, we can think of a case study simply as a short piece of drama. A forum theatre approach takes this text and encourages students to engage more critically and actively by stepping into the shoes of the 'characters' in the cases and by proposing their own solutions to the problems under discussion.

ACTIVE LEARNING AND PERFORMANCE: TIPS AND INSIGHTS FROM INTERVIEWEES

As Susan Maloney states in the quote at the beginning of this chapter, knowledge of a variety of performing arts skills enables us to engage others, and this is essential if our pedagogical approaches are learner-centred rather than didactic. The interviews with the teachers and performers provide some useful insights about how we can use performance to enhance the engagement and activity in our classrooms.

125

Teachers play a performative role but students are not our spectators

This first message about active learning and performativity leads on organically from Boal's Theatre of the Oppressed. Lindsay Masland talks about the importance of keeping in mind your performative role as a teacher whilst viewing your students as co-performers.

"But then there's also the piece of not viewing your students as an audience, but as other performers, artists, in the room, so it really depends on what you're doing on any day, because some days it's more effective for me to truly be a performer and a storyteller and get up there and give a straight 'performance'... But ...when we're trying to have the students do more of the work than we're doing, then you can't think of yourself as the performer- or as the person who is trying to deliver a true performance. So then you have to think of the students as the other actors on stage with you. And when I do that, I think about people I like to act with and be on stage with, it's actors who are very generous in terms of what they're giving to me so that I can give something back. So if I use that as a metaphor for teaching, it's like I need to be really generous to the students to give them something for them to be able to give something back to me."

Lindsay Masland, Interview 2

This sentiment is echoed by David Jay:

"I do also believe that teachers who see themselves exclusively as performers might be less able to promote inclusivity. Obviously, a crucial difference between a theatre audience and a class of students is that the former are generally more passive, and only occasionally identified as individuals. 'Performing' teachers who see their students as merely an audience to be entertained or inspired are perhaps less likely to adapt to individual needs and differences, even if they can empathise. That's why it's so important for teachers to remember that although performance is a major part of their job, it needs to be balanced with other approaches. If the classroom is seen as a theatre, teachers need to consider how to be stage directors as much as actors, if they really want to make individual learners into protagonists rather than mere spectators."

David Jay, Interview 4

In Boal's terms, the students are no longer passive spectators but instead are encouraged to be active spect-actors. However, Lindsay Masland draws our attention to the important point that active learning does not simply mean the teacher does less work or is less engaged. She talks about 'generosity' of performers on stage and transfers these thoughts to the teaching context. It is not sufficient to set up a task or a discussion; the teacher must still be present and must prepare the students for activity and interaction. In this way, active learning is not necessarily about students doing more and teachers doing less. The teacher still has an important role to play, and as David Jay points out, part of this role may be akin to a director in a theatre. The teacher is engaged in facilitating interactions and activities rather than delivering a didactic lecture 'in the spotlight'. This leads on to our second message about the groundwork that is needed in preparation for more active, performative classrooms.

Building trust and preparing students for active learning

As we noted above, in relation to the use of dramatic techniques such as forum theatre, there is an element of risk and uncertainty when trying to engage students in active learning. The success of a didactic lecture relies mainly on the teacher's own preparation and then delivery of the content. In contrast, active learning relies on complex negotiation of roles and interactions between several people. This, as Megan Bylsma points out, needs to be understood and acknowledged explicitly.

> "Students have to take risks. But students can only take those risks and be active in the classroom when they know the teacher has their back; when they know that the teacher has been taking risks, that the teacher understands that not all gambles pay out the way we hope, and that the point isn't the specific pre-planned answer at the end but the ways a person can say 'Yes, and' to get to the end of the journey and then examine all the things we've picked up on the way. To build a classroom where this kind of active learning takes place requires the teacher to have confidence that even if mistakes are made, they can be addressed at the end of the 'performance' and set right then. And it also requires a teacher who has prepared their students to feel safe taking such risks with their learning and, in the

students' minds, their grades. Creating that safety and trust is best done, in my experience, through team-building exercises that are rooted in an improv methodology. Setting students up for success, in my opinion, often requires they learn the basic ideas and tools of an improv troupe."

Megan Bylsma, Interview 8

At the heart of Megan Bylsma's perspective is trust. In the same way that a performer has to gain the trust of the audience, to inspire the audience to believe, and to be drawn in to the performance, a teacher must be able to create a learning environment in which students feel comfortable to engage with each other and to express themselves and their opinions. Megan Bylsma talks about improv as a useful way of creating such an environment. As we discussed in Chapter 6, the use of improv techniques can be useful for teachers to enhance the ability to think and act in the moment, and some of the improv games explained towards the end of Chapter 6 can help to break the ice and prepare students for more active, engaged, and interactive learning.

Enhancing speaking and listening skills: oracy and dialogic teaching

For stand-up comedian, Martin Billingham, a key link between active learning and performance is the development of speaking and listening skills – of students and of teachers.

"I've actually taught professors and lecturers, particularly scientists, about teaching being dialogic. There's a big push towards what's called oracy and dialogic learning. And what they really mean is speaking and listening."

Martin Billingham, Interview 6

Martin Billingham draws on the work of Robin Alexander, who outlines six key characteristics of a dialogic approach to teaching (Alexander 2017: 27–28):

- Collective: learning is a group endeavour, performed by students and teachers in collaboration.
- Reciprocal: ideas and counter-ideas are exchanged between students and teachers.

- Supportive: the teacher creates a learning environment in which ideas can be exchanged freely. This is similar to the non-judgmental ethos of 'yes, and' in improv games.
- Challenging: ideas can be challenged and questioned, and mistakes are a necessary and welcome part of the learning process.
- Cumulative: ideas are not generated in a vacuum; the collective and collaborative nature of dialogic teaching means that students and teachers build on each other's ideas.
- Purposeful: whilst dialogue should develop organically, there is still a purpose and level of structure to the interactions. The purpose of the dialogue is maintained and facilitated by the teacher.

Within this approach is a central focus on oracy. Martin Billingham talks about the complexity of developing effective speaking and listening skills, though this is not a simple matter of rhetoric: oracy is dialogic and interactive, not simply about transmitting a message from speaker to listeners. The work of Neil Mercer and colleagues at the University of Cambridge, though mainly in the primary and secondary education sectors, highlights the need for oracy as a 21st century skill (Littleton & Mercer 2013). This ability to perform and to communicate effectively in everyday situations is arguably more important than ever. Active learning provides a performative space for dialogue and oracy to flourish in ways that a didactic lecture simply does not. David Jay provides a practical performance-based exercise to help develop the teacher's own oracy:

"One further performance-based technique which I use when training new teachers, is 'scripting' instructions...Trainee teachers often struggle with limiting the amount and complexity of their talk, especially when giving instructions. To help them control this, they are encouraged to script simple and clear instructions before the lesson, and even rehearse them. This step, not dissimilar to an actor learning lines, allows them to ensure that their learners understand what is being asked of them."

David Jay, Interview 4

Clear instructions, which help students to engage in learning, do not happen by accident. Of course, students need to be free to develop their ideas and to engage in learning discussions which flow naturally. However, there needs to be an element of structure and planning on the part of the teacher, and the scripting exercise suggested by

David Jay is one way of ensuring the teacher's own spoken language is helpful to students in the learning context.

Keep tasks short, focused and active

A final lesson from performance is about the length and flow of activities. In my interview with Clare Chandler, a performer and musical theatre educator, she spoke about how she uses her performing experience to inform her planning of short, focused activities.

> "I tend to try and engage students in quite short and focused tasks. I'm mindful of my experience as a performer – that when you give an audience too much space, they don't always go where you want them to go. So keeping students engaged through varied questioning techniques. And if you're uncertain about things, acknowledge the uncertainty but not in a way that's apologetic. Make it more collaborative. Active learning is about being in charge of the space and the pace; being conscious that if energy is dwindling, knowing what else you can do or how you can motivate the students on to whatever the next task is."
>
> Clare Chandler, Interview 10

Clare Chandler compares performance, in which a key aim is to keep the audience engaged, with active learning, which has a similar aim. An important difference is that, in active learning, the teacher's role is to facilitate the activity and to promote interaction between students; the interactivity is multidirectional rather than a one-way engagement between audience member and performer. 'Being in charge of the space and the pace' emphasises the teacher's leadership role in facilitating active learning. Careful planning is clearly important, but it is also vital to be able to react in the moment to ensure that a task does not become too long, leading to disengagement. Clare Chandler talks about the ability to read body language – of audience members and of students – so that changes can be made – to the performance or the learning activity – in a spontaneous and dynamic way.

PERFORMANCE AS A TOOL TO PROMOTE INCLUSION

> Tell your story about learning. Ask them for their stories. Then transition into how the subject you are teaching impacts life.
>
> Kate Nasser, Interview 3

In our university classrooms, we are likely to have very diverse student populations, for example students of different ethnicities, genders, sexual orientations, from different socioeconomic backgrounds, and with a variety of individual needs and specific learning differences. Discussions about inclusivity were originally more prevalent in relation to children in primary and secondary school education, but as the diversity of students' needs in universities becomes more complex, research and conversations on this topic have shifted into the higher education sector (Moriña 2017).

The essence of inclusivity is that we focus on the inclusion of all rather than avoiding the exclusion of particular groups of students – a subtle but important difference. This distinction shifts the focus from barriers that a student might face – such as disability, language, culture – and emphasises instead that the teacher should strive to teach in ways that engage and include all students, regardless of any perceived barriers. In other words, a pedagogical decision which aims to include a student with a particular disability is likely also to be useful to learners who do not have this disability. The focus should therefore not be on the barrier – the excluding factor – but on the pedagogical solution which enables all to learn. Such solutions might relate to the practicalities of how you design your handouts, how you adapt your language to avoid idiomatic and slang expressions, or posting materials online a day or so before the class to give students time to prepare for the session. But how can performance, and the performative aspects that we have discussed in the previous chapters, help to promote an inclusive learning environment?

PAUSE FOR REFLECTION:

Reflect on your own experiences of being a student. Try to think of a teacher who was particularly successful at energising and engaging the whole class. What made this teacher successful at making you feel personally included and valued during the learning process?

It is likely that the teacher you were thinking of displayed many of the performative skills discussed throughout this book: paying attention to their use of voice, their body language, emitting an air of confidence, which in turn gives the students confidence to participate and to collaborate in the active learning space. In the context of actor training, Hanratty and McNamara (2020) draw our attention to important considerations of learning space design: in a traditional acting studio, the usual barriers between teacher and students (lectern, tables, laptops, etc.) do not exist. As the authors explain, such a space is more inclusive, as teachers and students are more integrated, and the focus is no longer on the teacher standing at the front of the classroom. The more flexible space of an acting studio is also more conducive to physical movement and the facilitation of active learning. Whilst teachers are unlikely to have (frequent) access to such performative learning spaces, it might be helpful to take inspiration from acting studios, for example, and to consider how more conventional classroom spaces might be (re)designed to be more inclusive and equitable.

Earlier in Chapters 5 and 6, we discussed how some of the techniques used by the famous Russian actor and director, Konstantin Stanislavski, might be adapted and applied to the teaching context. In particular, we looked at his concepts of motivation – asking questions about why a character behaves how she does – and the magic if – asking hypothetical but plausible questions about what you would do in certain situations. As a teacher, you can apply a similar technique to help understand the diverse needs, backgrounds, and motivations of your students. What do you need to know about your students in order to make your teaching more inclusive? What questions might you ask yourself? Some examples could be:

- How might the experiences and backgrounds (cultural, educational, socioeconomic, etc.) of my students influence their motivation, engagement, and learning in the classroom?
- How could I plan the session and activities to be more accessible to all students in my class?
- How could I adapt my style and performance to engage the different students in my classroom?
- What would I do if I were asked spontaneously to answer a question in front of the class?
- What would I do if I were not used to working in groups or engaging in highly interactive activities? How would I react to being asked to 'get into groups'?
- What would I do if I arrived at university hungry because I hadn't eaten since yesterday lunchtime?
- What would I do if I could not see myself (my ethnicity, gender, etc.) represented in the learning materials?

This technique of asking questions in order to get to know your students – or your character in a performance – is summed up nicely by Lindsay Masland:

> "The other thing about inclusivity is about understanding the students' context: who they are, where they're coming from, what their goals are, do they have family responsibilities- so good teaching and performance is about understanding context. You have to really know your students in order to be inclusive, and you do the same thing on stage."
>
> Lindsay Masland, Interview 2

Questions like this can help you not only to think about the various issues and needs your students might have, but also to consider how you might feel and react in those circumstances. This is the kind of empathy and understanding that an actor strives to develop for a character. Susan Maloney gives an example of how, as a teacher, activities can be scaffolded (cf. Bruner 1978) so that students feel able to participate even if they are more introverted:

> "I can relate to students who struggle with having the focus solely on them. I usually set up learning games, presentations and other in-class activities as small group or collective tasks so that each student can grow into different roles without the pressure of feeling unsupported or on show. I think if you can get everyone in the room active in some way rather than spectating, you already have a more inclusive space."
>
> Susan Maloney, Interview 5

The sample questions above are prompts to help you get to know your students; to empathise and to understand how you would feel and react if you were in their position. Empathy is a key theme that emerged from the interviews with many of the teachers and performers. For example, Anna McNamara talks about developing the art of storytelling as a means to promote empathy with other people's stories and situations:

> "Whatever we do, the human experience is about telling stories – our own stories, others' stories. And that's what researchers, lecturers and academics do essentially. They tell stories about their research.

Storytelling is the basic communication skill of a good teacher – or performer. If you can do this, you will be able to engage students in an active learning process. You will also be able to empathise with different people's stories and backgrounds, which enables you to design more inclusive learning experiences for your students. We have to think of ourselves as storytellers working with students who are also storytellers. They are not to be considered our audience, or consumers passively receiving a product. They're right in the narrative with us."

Anna McNamara, Interview 9

The thoughts here from Anna McNamara not only highlight the need for empathy and understanding, but this extract from the interview also brings us full circle to where we started in this chapter: in a classroom where students are learning actively, students are co-performers and co-creators of the learning that takes place. In this way, I would argue that active, collaborative learning, where the teacher makes use of performative skills to empathise with the students, can only lead to a more inclusive learning environment, in which all students feel able to participate.

REFERENCES AND FURTHER READING

Alexander, R. J. (2017) *Towards dialogic teaching: Rethinking classroom talk*, 5th ed. York: Dialogos.

Barnett, D. (2015) *Brecht in practice: Theatre, theory and performance.* London: Bloomsbury Methuen.

Boal, A. (2000) *Theater of the oppressed.* London: Pluto Press. New Edition. Transl. by C. Leal McBride, M-O. Leal McBride & E. Fryer.

Boal, A. (2002) *Games for actors and non-actors.* London: Routledge. Transl. by A. Jackson.

Bruner, J. S. (1978) The role of dialogue in language acquisition. In A. Sinclair, R. J. Jarvelle, & W. J. M. Levelt (eds.) *The Child's concept of language.* New York: Springer.

Chickering, A. & Gamson, Z. (1987) Seven principles for good practice in undergraduate education. *AAHE Bulletin* 39(7), 3–7.

Freeman, S., Eddy, S., McDonough, M., Smith, M., Okoroafor, N., Jordt, H., & Wenderoth, M. P. (2014) Active learning increases student performance in science, engineering and mathematics. *Proceedings of the National Academy of Science* 111(23), 8410–8415.

Freire, P. (1970) *Pedagogy of the oppressed.* New York: Seabury Press. Transl. by M. B. Ramos.

Hanratty, S. & McNamara, A. (2020) Student experience: Perspectives on learning in the university and the conservatoire. In: K. Gravett, N. Yakovchuk, & I. Kinchin (eds.) *Enhancing student-centred teaching in higher education: The landscape of student-staff research partnerships,* 31–44.

Howell Major, C., Harris, M. S., & Zakrajsek, T. (2016) *Teaching for learning: 101 Intentionally designed activities to put students on the path to success.* Oxford: Routledge.

Littleton, K. & Mercer, N. (2013) *Interthinking: Putting talk to work.* London: Routledge.

Moriña, A. (2017) Inclusive education in higher education: Challenges and opportunities. *European Journal for Special Needs Education* 32(1), 3–17.

Roberts, D. (2019) Higher education lectures: From passive to active learning via imagery? *Active Learning in Higher Education* 20(1), 63–77.

Timpson, W. & Burgoyne, S. (2014) *Teaching and performing: Ideas for energizing your classes,* 2nd ed. Madison: Atwood.

Unwin, S. (2014) *The complete Brecht toolkit.* London: Nick Hern.

Vygotsky, L. S. (1978) *Mind in society: The development of higher psychological processes.* Cambridge, MA: Harvard University Press.

Weimar, M. (2013) *Learner-centered teaching: Five key changes to practice,* 2nd ed. San Francisco: Jossey-Bass.

Wieman, C. (2014) Large-scale comparison of science teaching methods sends clear message. *Proceedings of the National Academy of Science* 111(23), 8319–8320.

Concluding remarks

Considering teaching as a performative activity offers one way of conceptualising what we do as educators in higher education. However, as David Jay points out, this model may not suit all teachers. Perhaps more important is the opportunity to reflect so that we can come to conclusions about the extent to which certain performative concepts, skills, and techniques resonate with us individually in our own teaching contexts.

> "Perhaps as part of a CPD session, ask teachers to reflect on similarities and differences between the classroom and the theatre, and on what that means to them specifically. As a trainer, I've noticed that while some teachers clearly relish the theatrical aspects, others have totally different approaches to teaching, for example seeing teaching as project management, or as therapeutic practice. I don't think the performance model suits everyone, but it's certainly an extremely valuable way of looking at teaching and learning."
>
> David Jay, Interview 4

Throughout this book, we have explored questions such as: to what extent can teaching be described as a performance? How do different types of performer present themselves confidently and engagingly? How do they overcome nerves and performance anxiety? What messages can teachers take from performers about how to create interactive, inclusive, and collaborative learning environments? We began in Chapter 1 by drawing on Goffman's notion of how we present ourselves differently in a variety of situations. To what extent do you present yourself differently as a teacher compared with when you are at home with your family, socialising with your friends, or just relaxing on your own at home? Do you have a persona that is specific to your teaching context(s)? The chapters in this book have hopefully prompted reflection on some of these questions, and presented some potential ways of drawing on the performing arts to enhance our confidence and performance as teachers.

FINAL REFLECTIONS AND ACTION POINTS

At various points throughout the book, you have been prompted to pause for reflection about the concepts, techniques, and exercises under discussion, and to consider how to use these within your own teaching context. The table below includes some final prompt questions to stimulate reflection on the various performance-related topics discussed throughout the book. Take a few moments to think about each topic and, if possible, write one or two action points for each topic, outlining how you intend to develop your practice in each area.

Final reflections and action points

Topic	Prompt Questions and Considerations
Teaching & performance	What similarities and differences do you see between teaching and performance? How would you describe your teaching persona? Are there any aspects of your teaching persona that you would like to change or develop?
Performance (teaching) anxiety	Do you ever get nervous or anxious about any aspects of your teaching? Which aspects in particular make you nervous? If there is more than one aspect, rank them starting from 1 as the most anxiety-inducing aspect. Which exercise(s) will you try out from those suggested in Chapter 3?
Voice	Summarise how you would describe your voice from the exercise in Chapter 4. For example, what is your average tempo? How loud is your normal speaking voice? What is your vocal range? How much of this range do you tend to use? What will you do to ensure you are taking care of your voice? Can you identify one area for development in relation to your voice? This might relate to your intonation and how you use stress and emphasis, or you might work on projecting your voice, for example. Which exercise(s) will you try out from those suggested in Chapter 4?

Final reflections and action points (continued)

Topic	Prompt Questions and Considerations
Body	How do you feel, physically, when you are teaching? Do you frequently have any areas of tension in your body? Are you aware of any gestures that you use frequently? To what extent do these gestures help you to communicate? What can you do to make your gestures more intentional? Which exercise(s) will you try out from those suggested in Chapter 5?
(Re)acting spontaneously & improvising	What kind of teacher are you in terms of preparation? Do you try to plan for all possible eventualities? Do you have a loose structure to your sessions? How do you portray yourself to your students? What is your 'status'? Which exercise(s) will you try out from those suggested in Chapter 6?
Active learning & inclusivity	What active learning methods do you frequently use with your students? Can you identify any aspects of performance that will help you to improve how you facilitate active learning with your students? Consider how you might adapt Boal's forum theatre technique for use in your own teaching context. What learning points will you take from performance about creating a more inclusive learning environment?

TOP PERFORMANCE TIPS

From your reflections while reading this book, you have hopefully thought about how some of the techniques and exercises from performance contexts might be adapted and applied to your teaching context. You may also have some ideas about how to develop the performative aspects of your teaching by thinking through the prompt questions in the table. I will conclude with some top tips for teaching from a performance perspective, all of which are inspired by the interviews with the teacher-performers.

Learn from others but be yourself, be authentic

The idea of authenticity brings us full circle to the beginning of Chapter 1, where I argued that to teach does not mean to act. Whilst we can learn from performers, teachers are not performing in the same way as an actor, who is playing a different character. We also discussed the idea of a teaching persona, and you may have reflected on how your teacher-self differs from your everyday self. It is important that this persona is believable so that you can build trust with your students. Having said this, you can also learn from others. You might have particular colleagues who become teaching role models for you. You might take inspiration from these colleagues, but imitating or attempting to impersonate others will lead to acting and inauthenticity.

"I think be authentic and be intentional. It's too easy in teaching to teach a certain way because that's how you were taught, or because you think your colleagues are expecting you to do that, but that doesn't mean learning is going to happen. So backwards design: think about your end goal and then you do everything with intentionality and authenticity to get there."

Lindsay Masland, Interview 2

"Being honest and authentic is key. So you're not really acting; you're being yourself. I talk a lot about the connection between thought, feeling and action. We cannot deliver anything in life authentically without these three elements being connected and in tune. We think, we feel, we do."

Anna McNamara, Interview 9

"[C]onsideration of status. When I observe some colleagues, they are sometimes limiting what they want to achieve because they either play, or enforce a status relationship that the students don't believe, so they inadvertently undermine themselves. As a performer, you are perhaps more aware of how you maintain a role consistently. There has to be an element of trust in the performer, or in the lecturer."

Clare Chandler, Interview 10

"[H]ave teaching heroes. This is something performers tend to do naturally – we have heroes who we watch and try to emulate. I guess teachers shouldn't aspire to actually be like someone else, but at least identifying people who inspire you – from a teaching performance perspective – observe them and try to take a little bit of what they have and incorporate it into your own style."

James Marples, Interview 7

139

Look for a kind set of eyes

In Chapter 3, we discussed the tendency that many of us have to allow self-doubt and negative thoughts to flourish. If we notice one bored face in a room of engaged students, many of us focus on the one person who looks disinterested, and this can make us nervous and negatively affect our performance. Sofia Alexiadou sums up nicely how we can help ourselves to focus instead on positivity in the classroom.

> "One thing from my experience as a teacher – I'm always looking for a kind set of eyes. You just see those students who are really engaged and every time you say something, their eyes just light up, you know. Even if you have a massive auditorium, even if you find two or three students that actually are really engaged with what you're saying, it boosts your performance. I just look for that polite set of eyes."
>
> Sofia Alexiadou, Interview 1

Get to know your voice

We devoted Chapter 4 to the teacher's most important tool: the voice. In most types of performance, the voice enables the performer to vary the ways in which messages are communicated to the audience. The same applies to teachers, and voice care is an important, but often overlooked, aspect of training in higher education teaching.

> "I would definitely advise all teachers to learn about their own voice, how to vary and project it for students' benefit, and, crucially, how to protect it. Just one training session on voice care can save a teacher from serious voice difficulties later in their career."
>
> David Jay, Interview 4

Get to know your students

We discussed at several points throughout the book the importance of collaboration and rapport between students and teachers. As Susan Maloney points out, getting to know your students – simply getting to know their names and a simple fact about them – can help to build rapport and can help to create a more inclusive learning environment where students are willing to engage and interact.

> "Try to get to know each student's name and one thing about them as you would when working with them on a performance or a

production. It charges you with the ability to give on the spot directions and gives you options to involve everyone in some way. Knowing a student's name and being able to call on them tells them that they matter regardless of the perceived size of their role."

Susan Maloney, Interview 5

Tell stories

A theme which arose at several points throughout the book was the art of storytelling. Telling stories is a vital communication skill and is perhaps one of the points where teaching and performance converge most strongly.

"[I]f you can develop your ability to tell stories, you will be able to engage your learners in active, collaborative learning. What does any good performer, teacher, author do? They communicate messages by telling good stories."

Anna McNamara, Interview 9

Take charge of the teaching space

An important aspect of the teacher's role is to create a safe and an engaging learning environment. Particularly in Chapter 3 in relation to stage fright and performance anxiety, we discussed the importance of becoming familiar with – taking charge of – the teaching space as a way of increasing confidence.

"[T]ake charge of the furniture, and I mean the whole teaching space and the atmosphere in the space. I think the more you do this, the more it puts you in command of the situation."

James Marples, Interview 7

Turn problems into opportunities

One of the most common anxieties about performance, and also among teachers, is how to deal with the unexpected. We discussed, particularly in Chapter 6, what we might learn from improvisation. One of the key aspects of live performance is that things can 'go wrong' or 'off script', and the same applies to teaching. A certain amount of planning can help to cope with unplanned problems. However, it is perhaps more useful to develop a mindset that turns potential mishaps into learning and teaching opportunities.

" '[T]he obstacle is the way'. Use the real, in-the-moment things to your advantage. The things that we see as a problem or a distraction can be turned into something useful. And I think if you think along these lines, you're likely to be less anxious, or have less stage fright, about things potentially going wrong. Those are also the moments that people, or your students, are likely to remember."

James Marples, Interview 7

Be daring – try things out!

Depending on your perspective on teaching and performance, some of the exercises and techniques discussed throughout this book may seem daunting, or just strange! This final tip is about keeping an open mind and giving yourself permission to take risks, even if you are not convinced that teaching is a performative activity.

"[O]ne thing I think – and I tell people who I train – is to just do it! Things are never as bad as you think. Specifically in the teaching context, it's important to make that personal connection with your students; greet them personally at the door. It completely changes the dynamic in the room."

Martin Billingham, Interview 6

"Get out of your head! ... Come to terms with the fact that each class is a performance. Higher education teachers could hate this concept as it seems to imply 'edutainment' instead of education. However, instead see it as something that is already part of your role whether you like it or not and something you can get better at. Performers know that practice and trying out new things is the way to gain great performances. And sometimes a performance is really not good, but that's just fuel to feed your next performance to make it so much better."

Megan Bylsma, Interview 8

"Lighten it up. It breaks tension. It allows people to laugh and have an "I enjoyed that" memory connected to your class. They willingly come back for more and become more active once they get there."

Kate Nasser, Interview 3

THE END

This brings us to the end of our discussion about teaching as a performative activity. Depending on where you were in your thinking when you began reading the book, I hope to have at least prompted some reflection on what we do as teachers in higher education, or perhaps more precisely, *how* we perform our role as teachers. And even more importantly, how enhancing our performance can help us to fulfil our central aim as educators: to facilitate students' learning. If paying attention to the performative aspects of our teaching leads, as a happy side effect, to increased enjoyment and entertainment, for our students and for ourselves, this is all the better.

Appendix

INTERVIEW 1: SOFIA ALEXIADOU

RB: Can you say a bit about your teaching and performance background?

SA: I'm Sofia, I'm a lighting designer and I teach lighting design and video design for LIPA. I'm a practising lighting designer, which means I do shows outside my academic life, which is quite interesting because we are a performing arts institute, which means we do shows, so we have to keep up with industry.

RB: So they are very much applied courses?

SA: Yeah, it's the same as doctors, I would say. How can you teach surgery without being a surgeon, you know what I'm saying, it's very practical, not just about the theory, what we do, so I think it's really interesting for me to be a teacher and a practitioner at the same time. I think they feed each other, if it makes sense. So I've been teaching at LIPA for the past five years. I'm about to finish my PhD, which is again, a more theoretical approach to lighting design; it's the history of lighting design in Greece, so that's it really.

RB: So you're coming to the end of your PhD?

SA: Yeah, I had a funny way to teaching actually. My first BA was in Italian language and literature, and then I did an MA in Translation and a second MA in Theatre Studies, and it's funny because now I'm doing an MA – and I promise this is the last one I'm ever going to do – which is in Management so it's quite interesting because the HE sector in the UK is changing rapidly. In terms of performing experience – I have never been an actress but I work with them quite a lot so I can understand them; I can see how they approach their work.

RB: So you have quite a lengthy teaching experience. To what extent do you see teaching as a kind of performance?

SA: Well, the first and most obvious thing is that you are not yourself; you are performing as the teacher, the lecturer, that's the very first thing. I never find myself being myself when I'm teaching because I'm just wearing a different hat, so I'm sort of teaching them via the role they think I am playing. And I'm quite different because I come from a different culture; I'm discussing things that they wouldn't normally be discussing, like European theatre, which in the UK is totally absent, they don't have any connection to that. So I think the first thing is that I am playing a role, I'm not really a teacher, and because we are discussing performance, in a way, in order to make my point, I think the way I'm approaching the lecture in the classroom is that there is the beginning and an end to the lecture, but for sure I think I'm following the structure of a proper play, if that makes sense. At the very end, there is a resolution to the lecture. In that way I see teaching as performance really. We do teaching observations every year and I can see other lecturers and how they approach that; there are different types of actors as well, you know. Students need everything; they need a provocative role, which is where I am. And they need somebody who has a steady approach to sound, let's say, so I think it's a good thing for them to have a variety of approaches.

RB: And I'm writing a bit about stage fright and performance anxiety, partly because teachers I talk to often speak about being nervous and I kind of link that to performance and stage fright. Is that something you can relate to, or you see that in other people?

SA: Yeah, I think for me that was a bit tricky during my first year, I would say, but then... it's quite different because we are sort of a smaller uni, I would never teach a class with more than 40 students, and I have classes with just 4 or 5 of them, so I don't think we are the same as colleagues who go into big auditoriums with 500 students, so I would say the first year was a bit tricky for me, only because I had to make sure that the structure of my lectures could actually hit the learning outcomes of the module, so that was the thing for me – am I teaching them what I should be teaching them? But yeah, I can see other colleagues – they cannot stand in front of a class and deliver a lecture. It's a muscle you have to exercise, and I think it's a personality thing.

145

RB: And I had a question about active learning, getting students actively engaged, and I guess in your kind of work it's all very much active because it's a practical topic.

SA: Yeah, the first thing I'm saying to them – my way of teaching can never work if they don't engage, because I'm not really teaching them; I have this funny system where I'm just trying to get into their heads and understand how they see what I'm showing them, so yeah, I don't have lectures where I just talk. For me that's a pointless lecture, actually. You don't progress, personally as a teacher.

RB: So I'm wondering to what extent just being aware as a teacher of performance and performing arts skills that you might use in singing, acting, whatever else – whether honing these skills as a teacher can help to make your teaching more active?

SA: Richard, I think that's a given, you know. For us, I think we should be doing something like a PG Cert to proper lecturers because – if you see the acting department, the music department – if you see the lecturers there – I think theatre is actually feeding our teaching practice. There is a gap there in the industry; we could actually be giving small talks on this – you know because it is acting – when you stand in front of an audience, whether that's theatre or the classroom, you are still performing, so I think there's a gap in the industry there that we could cover – in short sessions with colleagues from other unis where we can discuss those things.

RB: Yeah, I think some universities do have the odd short course on various aspects of performance, but there's little as far as I can see that is really coherent, which I think people like you could be developing as part of a course such as a PG Cert, a PG Diploma rather than one-off courses.

SA: I think it's really going through a funny phase. I can see that from the past two or three years with the funding situation, it's just – we are moving towards more dynamic schemes of teaching or co-delivering you know, in a way now all of a sudden we are discussing whether we can co-deliver some modules with the acting department, which is interesting because I'm teaching a technical theatre course, so it's a very funny way of bringing both together. And I think that's where every uni will go – a revalidating period of changing their – most lecturers are going to find themselves teaching stuff they wouldn't normally be teaching, you know.

RB: I have a question – I imagine from your name, are you Greek?

SA: Yes, I'm Greek.

RB: I wonder whether there are any different performance anxieties experienced by teachers whose first language isn't English?

SA: Massively! During my first year, I had a thing about whether they could understand my accent, you know, and that was making me even more anxious at times. Or the fact that I couldn't get really heavy accents, like the Scouse accent.

I cannot be less Greek; I am thinking in Greek; I think the structure of my sentences is different really because the Greek language is very visual. It has a very rich vocabulary. I was saying to the students – you don't need any subtext because the words are so heavy, but with English there is a lot of subtext and sometimes I don't understand the subtext, and that's a barrier for me with my students as well. You know, they are so held back because of their culture. I mean if you want to discuss in theatre terms – the fourth wall is there because of the subtext, you know, so my worry is trying to pull that wall down for them. Because of the system in the UK, they are expecting me to tell them what to do, which is for me exactly the opposite, I just want to see what they can do and then I can work with them. Yeah, for sure, the language thing was a big thing for me in the beginning, really big and made me really anxious.

RB: Yeah, I can relate to that because I've taught in German-speaking countries so I have experienced it the other way round. And as you said, the issue wasn't just your own language but also about responding to other students when they're speaking English and trying to understand them.

SA: Yes, I see that sometimes, for example with some of my students who are non-native English speakers, they are really struggling, you know, and I can see that that's something that is keeping them in isolation; they don't interact because they don't feel safe that they would be understood, so all of a sudden they create this bubble and then just protect themselves. So how do you work around that if someone isn't really talking because they can't really express themselves – so yeah, it's a big thing.

RB: Linked to that is the issue of inclusivity. If you're a teacher who is much more aware of yourself and you can 'perform,' perhaps you can bring the students in and engage them more and make the classroom more inclusive.

SA: I think it's true. When I was doing the PG Cert – there is a framework, you can apply certain techniques. The thing with my students is that they come from really diverse backgrounds, which means that because we have a practical course, the skill set that they have when they begin the BA is massively different, so all of a sudden I have to bridge the gap in knowledge, you know, so in order to do that you have to make the weaker students come closer to you and in a way find attributes that you have that they can identify in themselves – so sort of a role – I mean that's the whole thing about theatre and performance, I mean you identify yourself as that person on stage; therefore, you're more empathetic. So that's what I'm trying to do; I'm trying to show them my weaknesses because people like you when you open your cracks and you just go 'I'm a human being as well' – but then again as a teacher you have to move between those two things: that you are the 'authority' and at the same time a human being, so I think that balance is something that can keep everybody engaged in the classroom.

RB: Yeah, you said something earlier about getting into their heads. I think that's an interesting inclusivity point. If you can get into their heads and understand where they're coming from, their cultural background, their experiences outside class, then I suppose you can almost – if you're an actor – kind of studying a role – you're almost studying your students in that way and you can adapt your teaching to them to make it more inclusive.

SA: Yeah, for sure, and I teach different year groups differently. Some of my students have been more dynamic, so all of a sudden I have to be more robust; some other year groups have been more quiet so I have to just adapt the way I'm teaching according to my audience.

RB: And I think – final thing – do you have any advice or tips for higher education teachers about anything related to performance?

SA: One thing from my experience as a teacher – I'm always looking for a kind set of eyes. You just see those students who are really engaged and every time you say something, their eyes just light up, you know. Even if you have a massive auditorium, even if you find two or three students that actually are really engaged with what you're saying, it boosts your performance. I just look for that polite set of eyes.

RB: That's something I can definitely relate to. Polite set of eyes, that's a really nice way of putting it.

SA: Yeah, a couple of years ago, I had a student who seemed really disengaged. But it was my mistake because I waited until the end of the module to ask her about this, and when I did, she opened up and had massive problems with her family, so it wasn't me. If I had asked her really early on, I would have tried to find another way of keeping her engaged in the classroom. Because we tend to forget that they're human beings as well; they're not just vessels that we fill with knowledge; they have problems. And most of the times the 'negativity' from them is not about you.

RB: Yes, and in some ways, talking about teaching as a performance puts you as a teacher at the centre, but actually it's not always about you. As you've said, there could be a problem in a student's private life, so it's making sure you don't make it all about you, I suppose, as the teacher.

SA: Yeah, I think it would be interesting if you examine as well the different types of performance we now have because we are discussing more and more about immersive theatre, so I mean when I was studying it was sort of a performance with the lecturer – it was a one-way thing; he was just feeding us. But now I think it's more like immersive theatre, you know.

    I was just in Berlin and got a really amazing book. It's called *Audience Participation in Theatre.* It says "The 19th century was a century of actors, the 20th a century of directors, the 21st a century of spectators." And I think it's true. You have performances where the audience are actually creating the show, so I think that's where we are right now.

RB: Great, thank you very much.

INTERVIEW 2: LINDSAY MASLAND

RB: Can you just say a bit about who you are, your teaching and performance background?

LM: OK, my name is Lindsay Masland and I live in the United States, North Carolina. I teach at a university so we offer both undergraduate education and we have some Master's and doctoral degrees. I started teaching at this university in 2011 right after finishing my PhD, which is in educational psychology and also statistics, so I guess that's eight years of teaching, and I just got tenure last year. I mostly teach future teachers, both those who are planning on teaching 5-18 year olds, K-12 – so when I'm teaching them, they normally have to take one psychology class as a part of their degree regardless of the type of teaching they want to do. And then I also do some graduate teaching for people who want to be school psychologists. So I teach them an introduction class and then also a statistics class; how to use statistics in school settings. And then I also teach our graduate teaching assistants. They have a three-course sequence they have to take before they're allowed to teach as graduate students and then once they receive a teaching position, they have to continue receiving training and I provide all that. So that's what I teach. And then in terms of performance, my main things are dance and musical theatre. I started those things, well dance when I was three years old and I hated it! I was a very academic child and did a lot of reading. But my mom told me I had to pick an extra-curricular activity to do while my brother was at baseball. One of the activities was jazz dance. So I went in there and we were told that our recital was going to be songs from *Greece*, and I had never really seen that dancing and singing could be something that happened together, and that dancing could be something other than just ballet. So once I saw that, I was like, "oh, OK, I'm happy about this" and so I auditioned for the main part in our show and got it, and from then on I was committed. And then I started learning to appreciate ballet and all the other forms, but theatre was really the thing that got me into it. So I did that all throughout high school, college as an extra-curricular activity – started focusing a lot on tap dancing actually – and then had kids, and stopped for about 10 years. Then a new dance studio opened here in town with offerings for adults. So I picked it up again four or five years ago, and got back into musical the-atre after a 10-year break, so now I do musical theatre again and I am the dance captain, assistant director, for a dance company that dances in the style of the Rockettes – the high kicking and tapping – so we have a company of 25 girls and women. It's very much about precision and everyone doing the same moves. So that's what I do now.

RB: Very cool. So the next question is really to what extent do you see a link between teaching and performance?

LM: Well I think for a long time I tried to keep them very separate. I think I was raised to believe that performance and artistic endeavours are extra-curricular and then academics are your real job – I mean my parents weren't academics but just in terms of what kids are supposed to be doing with themselves. I think I unintentionally carried that with me into my career. So I think I was trying to be more serious – and you can tell I'm not serious, but I was trying to come across as this serious academic, and that's probably the reason why I added statistics to my PhD. So I'm short, I'm a woman, I have a lot of energy, and that package right there already makes people not take me as seriously, and I think because I was good at math, I added that on because people take that more seriously. So I think I kept them separate for a while and tried not to bring too much performance into the classroom because I was thinking I might dilute the effects of what I was trying to achieve, so thinking of everything very scientifically, and I still do, but then when I started getting back into theatre, I started seeing performance bleeding into the classroom in really nice ways, and started dropping the whole intention to keep teaching and performance separate and am probably more theatrical than ever before, and it's great! So I think the most obvious way that teaching is performance are the moments when you're sage on the stage and people are looking at you; it feels like a performance, that's pretty obvious, but different performers view what they're doing on the stage differently. Some performers are trying to take the artist's work and stay as true as possible to the work and understand the artist's motivation, but I'm less of that kind of performer and teacher. To me it's more about: what kind of experience do I want the audience to have – or the students? So it's really about backwards designing not only my courses but also my performance. If I think about who's in the audience that changes the qualities that are necessary out of me as a performer. So I think, me being really clear on what I want my audience, or my students, to get out of the experience and design it from there. But then there's also the piece of not viewing your students as an audience, but as other performers, artists, in the room, so it really depends on what you're doing on any day, because some days it's more effective for me to truly be a performer and a storyteller and get up there and give a straight 'performance.' In fact those are the things that students seem to talk about on evaluations, and if I run into them five years later, that's what they remember. So clearly that's effective. But, and this gets into your question about active learning, when we're trying to have the students do more of the work than we're doing, then you can't think of yourself as the performer – or as the person who is trying to deliver a true performance. So then you have to think of the students as the other actors on stage with you. And when I do that, I think about people I like to act with and be on stage with, it's actors who are very generous in terms of what they're giving to me so that I can give something back. So if I use that as a metaphor for teaching, it's like I need to be really generous to the students to give them something for them to be able to give something back to me. So I say those are the two ways: being a performer and then seeing the students as an audience and as co-actors. And depending on what your learning objectives are, you're gonna go back and forth between those.

RB: It's interesting you were saying before about separating teaching and performance. I suppose in some ways, when you were doing that, you were actually still in some ways more of a performer, because you were acting, trying to act serious, I suppose in some ways you were acting a part that wasn't really you so much. And I say in the book, partly from theoretical underpinning and partly from my own opinion, that I don't think it's helpful if we say teachers are actors; people might be put off or intimidated by that, but I think the way you started by saying you were separating teaching and performance and putting on this act of someone really serious and academic, maybe that was more of an act, but now maybe you're using more of your performance skills but being more yourself, perhaps?

LM: Well yeah, that's interesting because, for your last question about top tips, the thing that I wrote down was above all be authentic, right, and that's kind of what you're saying, that before I wasn't being as authentic as I could, and now I am and I'm probably more effective as a result, because even with art or performance, there's not one right way to perform a piece, and if you think that, you won't be a very good actor. And in the same way, if you think there's one right way to teach a thing, then you're not gonna be as good a teacher. The most important thing is to think about the interactions between all the players, whether we're talking about stage or classroom, we've got the material, which is what is to be taught or what is to be shared with the audience; we've got the person who's delivering that, which is the teacher or the performer, and then we've got the audience, which is the audience or the students, and if you only think about one of those things, it's not gonna be as good. But if you think about how all of those things interact – I might make certain choices as an actor or as a teacher that are great when they come out of me. But if I tell the person in the office next to me to do that, it's gonna fall flat because that's not who they are. You know sometimes I'll just get on the table if the story calls for it. But there's a lot of colleagues I would never tell to climb on the table. But for me, I have a lot of energy and run around the classroom and stuff, so it's not weird if I then jump on the table. So I agree, we don't need to tell people to do x, y, z, because it's really about who you are and how you interact with the content and with the students.

RB: Great, so the next question is about stage fright, performance anxiety, teacher anxiety. Is this something you've experienced in either role as a teacher or a performer?

LM: So this is a hard question for me because I don't get stage fright. I think it's just some kind of natural predisposition. My view as a psychologist is that our genetics set some upper, lower bounds of the most stage fright and least stage fright you're going to experience, or the most extrovert and the least extrovert – these genetic bounds, but then there's a lot of space for movement in between, so if you're someone who has some kind of predisposition to have stage fright, I think the way to view that is to say sure, but we can move ourselves to a point of having the least amount of stage fright. But also as a psychologist, I guess I would say that stage fright is essentially anxiety bound to a specific context and, for a lot of people, it's tied to fear of messing up. But the other thing we know too is that we usually give our best performances in the context of anxiety. So thinking about stage fright as something that we need to completely get rid of is not a very adaptive way to think about it. We actually do worse if we have zero anxiety. So you can actually think of it as a point of power instead of a point of weakness. So, I do get nervous – not before I teach my students – maybe in my first year, but now I have 50 students in the room at most and then 8 at least, so I'm not in front of hundreds of students at once.

RB: And do you notice any difference between teaching 50 people and 8 people?

LM: That's a good question. Actually I feel more stage fright in the 8-person scenario, because for me it's more natural to do the performance thing, and the more faces there are, the more it becomes a sea of not real people. So I get more anxious about the smaller classes, probably because those are the ones that will require more improv, right, because in a smaller class there's an expectation that there's going to be much more give and take between the students and the teachers. And you don't know what's going to happen. Whereas in a big group, it's a lot more predictable, even if you have active learning, I feel like it's more predictable in that context.

RB: Again, I find it interesting that you find it more nerve racking with a smaller group because actors often say they're quite shy people and that they find it harder interacting with a small group than with a theatre full of people. It sounds similar to your experience.

LM: It's true. I've always been told I'm an extrovert, and it's true that I can talk easily, but about things I want to talk about. So if we're having a dinner party, and the topic that we're going to discuss is x, then I'm happy. So I don't feel like a very good improv person.

RB: That kind of links to the next question about using performing arts skills in teaching. Is there anything you think you bring into your teaching, either subconsciously, or having reflected, things that you do knowingly?

LM: I think it was mostly not consciously for a while. But because it was who I am, it was coming in anyway. I've always got good student evaluations – and I'm not saying that to boast – you can be entertaining and have zero learning occur – so being entertained is not that important, but I think the reason I have been entertaining is because I have had years of practising these skills, being on stage and just getting really comfortable. So one thing that made this really clear to me was watching one of my friends present at a conference and he was talking about his process and how he even thinks about things like where he will be standing when he delivers certain pieces of information. And the tone of voice that he will use. And this made me realise: we can do that! It really gave me the permission to start doing that intentionally. So I guess in terms of specific things I'm doing: using props to get points across, thinking about where I'm standing when I'm saying certain things, thinking about it all in stories. Tone of voice – I'll whisper, and shout at certain times. But if that's not natural for you, that might feel a little awkward. So I think the most important thing is developing storytelling techniques. Think about how you already naturally tell stories and then bring that into your teaching. I think another thing is watching the students' faces really carefully. Then I play off that. I think of them as the actors giving me an emotion. If I see someone confused, I ask what they're confused about, so that's also improv.

RB: And you mentioned it before in relation to active learning, and I think this also helps to bring the students into the 'production,' by reading their faces.

LM: Yeah, and also if you're doing anything that's not direct instruction, you as the teacher are not the main reference point anymore, but I still think there's a place for performance. In my experience, students would rather sit and listen to a lecture, particularly if it's an entertaining lecture, but we know that if we want learning to happen, we have to be intentional for that kind of instruction. And I've found that it really works with buy in: getting them to do this active stuff. If I've spent time to be really engaging, they'll kind of do whatever I ask them to do. And this connects to your question about inclusivity. So if you look at my student evaluations, the thing people say is that I'm entertaining – or some word it like that – but they also say 'she's really hard.' And that's what I want them to say, because I've done whatever's needed to make them work hard, or to accept really tough criticism of their work.

RB: I think that's a really good point, a kind of trade off. You said before about being generous, so you are generous in your performance and giving students something fun and engaging and then they're more willing to engage in return.

LM: Yeah, and the other thing about inclusivity is about understanding the students' context: who they are, where they're coming from, what their goals are, do they have family responsibilities – so good teaching and performance is about understanding context. You have to really know your students in order to be inclusive, and you do the same thing on stage.

RB: Yes, that's what I was thinking with that question. As an actor, you have to get to know a character. So as a teacher, you have to get to know your students.

LM: Yeah, when I think in terms of statistics, we have this outcome variable, this dependent variable which is learning. We can measure this in lots of different ways, but that's the goal. Then we have an independent variable, the thing we're manipulating, which is our teaching. So we have an intervention, which is teaching, and an outcome, which is learning. But if that's all you think about, sometimes you do something that should work, but nothing happens. I guess you could blame it on the students. But in science, we never just look at dependent and independent variables. What else is going on that's going to make my intervention more effective? So the feelings and context of students are just another package of variables that we have to attend to as teachers.

RB: Great, so just to finish, you already mentioned one top tip. Do you have any other top tips for teachers?

LM: So yeah, I think be authentic and be intentional. It's too easy in teaching to teach a certain way because that's how you were taught, or because you think your colleagues are expecting you to do that, but that doesn't mean learning is going to happen. So backwards design: think about your end goal and then you do everything with intentionality and authenticity to get there.

RB: Great, thank you very much.

INTERVIEW 3: KATE NASSER

*Responses submitted in writing.

RB: Can you introduce yourself briefly?

KN: I was already a trained teacher, teaching for a living, when I discovered my performance ability (acting, singing, dancing). It became crystal clear that beyond performing on stage for audiences, performance techniques were enhancing my teaching. In fact, it was my sister (an academic) who watched me teach one day and said later 'it was like watching a one-woman show.'

RB: In what ways do you see teaching as performance?

KN: Teaching is about reaching people with your subject. Performance is about reaching people with your message. The challenge for many teachers is that they see teaching as real and serious and they see performance as fake and flighty. Yet they are the same. "You must reach them to teach them."

Personal example: One day I was slated to teach the same session in the morning and the afternoon. The previous night I had a very upsetting experience. I was struggling in the morning even to maintain my composure. So I closed down my emotions completely and gave a straight lecture session. Reviews of the session were bad. It was horrible. During lunch I was reeling from the embarrassment of the morning debacle. I said to myself, "Enough of this. Go for it like you know you can."

I taught the afternoon session (same exact material) with my true performance ability. The reviews were outstanding. If you have ever thought that *how you teach* doesn't matter, think again. It matters. You are teaching people of different ages, personality types, cultures, background, and goals. "Reach them to teach them."

RB: Do you ever experience stage fright or performance anxiety – on stage and/or in your work as a teacher? If so, how do you manage this?

KN: Yes I have had both stage fright and classroom fright. Classroom fright is easier to overcome. Just walk around and talk to the students *before* you start teaching. As they enter the room, be among them. When you talk one-on-one, everyone starts to feel that it's normal human interaction. When I am doing a show, it's rarely possible to talk to the audience before the curtain goes up. So when I feel the butterflies, I direct the energy into a wider and wider smile back stage. If there is a mirror, look at yourself smiling this energy. Now you're ready to perform for others.

RB: Do you use any of the skills from your work as a performer to enhance your performance in your teaching role? If so, how do you do this?

KN: Voice tone – yes. It is the simplest mechanism to lend meaning and emphasis to words. Louder, softer, pitch, pace, pauses – all create a story telling ambiance that draws people in.

I am big on body language but not all my body language is big. When you let your natural body language emerge, it communicates so much more than words. On the other hand, if you 'learn' body language, it may seem fake. Also, if all your body language is big and bold, people become numb to it. Think 'variation' as the true influencing power of voice tone and body language.

RB: To what extent do you think performing arts techniques can help to promote active learning in the classroom?

KN: To put it simply, performance awakens people's interest, curiosity, and thinking (as well as their emotions, soul, etc...). Regardless of your subject matter, if you want students to do something more than sit and listen, you must ignite that something. Take time in advance of your class to list out what you want them to actively do. Then picture how to make that happen.

RB: How can an enhanced teaching performance promote inclusivity in learning?

157

KN: Story telling! Tell your story about learning. Ask them for their stories. Then transition into how the subject you are teaching impacts life. Get their views. Even technical subjects can be taught this way.

RB: Do you have any top tips for higher education teachers about how they can enhance their performance in the teacher role?

KN: Step One: If you find the idea of performance as anathema to your work as a professor in higher education, rethink the word performance. I see it more as effective influencing. Consider how great lawyers over the centuries pleaded their clients' cases. Think about how auspicious debate teams in great institutions of higher learning have spoken with great conviction. Powerful orators have taught many people philosophy of life. Gurus have moved people to revolutionary change. It's about reaching people to help them in some way. You can do it to help students learn.

Remember that you are teaching people. Some are auditory learners but many need you to engage their multiple senses and needs to become truly engaged in your topic.

Step Two: Lighten it up. It breaks tension. It allows people to laugh and have an 'I enjoyed that' memory connected to your class. They willingly come back for more and become more active once they get there.

INTERVIEW 4: DAVID JAY

*Responses submitted in writing.

RB: Can you introduce yourself briefly?

DJ: I've been teaching and training for around 20 years. I started in EFL teaching, then developed experience in HE as an EAP tutor, teacher trainer, and lecturer on degree modules in linguistics at Anglia Ruskin University, where I've worked for the past six years. Most recently, I have been involved in research into classroom management and how communicative methods can be adapted for HE teaching in different disciplines including science, nursing, and business management.

Before becoming a teacher I worked for three years in artist management. I worked for agencies in London and Italy, representing international opera singers, and was always fascinated by the psychology of performers, for example how they faced the pressures of going on stage and how they expressed emotions, both on and off stage. Although I don't work in the arts nowadays, I'm a keen amateur singer and perform with the Cambridge Rock Choir!

RB: In what ways do you see teaching as performance?

DJ: The connection between teaching and performance first became clear to me when studying Brecht's *Lehrstücke* or 'teaching plays' for German A-level. His approach to theatre made me wonder whether dramatists should see themselves as teachers as well as entertainers. I liked the idea that going to the theatre should always provide some sort of educational benefit for the audience, be it spiritual, moral, or academic. When I became a teacher, the idea of performance continued to interest me. As well as putting on plays and drama events with EFL learners in my earlier teaching days, I've often used drama activities in class (e.g. role plays, or actors' warm-ups before speaking activities), as a way of developing students' confidence. They seem to feel comfortable taking on another 'persona' which allows them to overcome shyness and/or 'blocks' in using new language. As a learner of Italian, I found that using another language seemed to allow me to express myself in ways that I couldn't previously, even in English.

More recently, I've found that thinking of the classroom as theatre can be helpful in teacher training. In my recent research project (*No Drama? Two theatrical strategies for initial teacher training*, presented at IATEFL Brighton 2018), I looked at how basic principles from theatre/choreography can be used to help new teachers develop their classroom management. Another strand of the same presentation was about 'good' and 'bad' theatricality: as a teacher trainer and observer, I do also feel that theatricality can have a negative effect on teaching and learning, if it isn't channelled properly. For example, I've quite often seen novice (and indeed experienced) teachers using a theatrical teacher presence simply to entertain learners, 'playing to the gallery' without really fostering learning at a deeper level. That's something I encourage trainee teachers to be aware of, and avoid.

RB: Do you ever experience stage fright or performance anxiety – on stage and/or in your work as a teacher? If so, how do you manage this?

DJ: This may sound strange, but as long as I feel prepared for whatever it is I am going to perform or teach, I don't feel anxious at all. In fact, going on stage – or into the classroom to

teach – usually gives me a positive 'buzz' which is addictive!
I have given lectures and sung solo in front of quite large audiences and thoroughly enjoy it. I do need to focus before a performance, and get a feeling of anticipation beforehand, but I don't think I've ever experienced stage fright or performance anxiety. The only time I get nervous is if I feel I'm not fully prepared or comfortable with the subject matter, be it lesson content or the music/lyrics. For that reason I like to prepare/rehearse thoroughly before any lesson or performance and I encourage trainee teachers to do the same. If there is a feeling of anxiety it usually comes a few days beforehand when I'm preparing and trying to get everything to the right standard, so I can then enjoy the 'performance' on the day itself.

RB: Do you use any of the skills from your work as a performer to enhance your performance in your teaching role? If so, how?

DJ: Learning to support my voice using the breath/diaphragm for singing was directly transferable to the classroom as it helped me to project my voice audibly without straining it. That helped me survive a period of voice strain, which hasn't recurred since. Studying singing also made me more aware of how listening to other people's voices can give clues to their underlying emotions and level of confidence, which definitely helps with empathy, both as a teacher and trainer. I'm not a trained actor but I do remember and use techniques from my school and university acting days, like not turning one's back on the audience, or being aware of body position and how affects rapport. From the occasional dance class I have attended, I got the idea of numbered positions, which I applied to teacher training in the *No Drama?* project, as above.

One further performance-based technique which I use when training new teachers, is 'scripting' instructions. This is of course widely used, especially in language teaching, where teachers need to ensure that their own talk in the 'target' language is accessible to learners. Trainee teachers often struggle with limiting the amount and complexity of their talk, especially when giving instructions. To help them control this, they are encouraged to script simple and clear instructions before the lesson, and even rehearse them. This step, not dissimilar to an actor learning lines, allows them to ensure that their learners understand what is being asked of them. Obviously, scripting instructions for every lesson would be excessively time-consuming; the scripting isn't usually needed after a few practice lessons, as clear instructions often start to come naturally.

RB: How can an enhanced teaching performance promote inclusivity in learning?

DJ: I think that an awareness of the vocal and emotional challenges of speaking in front of an audience can help teachers support all learners. However, I do also believe that teachers who see themselves exclusively as performers might be less able to promote inclusivity. Obviously, a crucial difference between a theatre audience and a class of students is that the former are generally more passive, and only occasionally identified as individuals. 'Performing' teachers who see their students as merely an audience to be entertained or inspired are perhaps less likely to adapt to individual needs and differences, even if they can empathise. That's why it's so important for teachers to remember that although performance is a major part of their job, it needs to be balanced with other approaches. If the classroom is seen as a theatre, teachers need to consider how to be stage directors as much as actors, if they really want to make individual learner into protagonists rather than mere spectators.

RB: Do you have any top tips for higher education teachers about how they can enhance their performance in the teacher role?

DJ: Firstly, I would definitely advise all teachers to learn about their own voice, how to vary and project it for students' benefit, and, crucially, how to protect it. Just one training session on voice care can save a teacher from serious voice difficulties later in their career.

For a higher education context, I would say teachers/lecturers should look closely at the module outcomes and consider what students on this module will really need. If there are performative elements, like a presentation or seminar-based assessment, use directorial techniques to support students as protagonists. If not, still consider how theatrical techniques can inspire the students and facilitate their learning.

Perhaps as part of a CPD session, ask teachers to reflect on similarities and differences between the classroom and the theatre, and on what that means to them specifically. As a trainer, I've noticed that while some teachers clearly relish the theatrical aspects, others have totally different approaches to teaching, for example seeing teaching as project management, or as therapeutic practice. I don't think the performance model suits everyone, but it's certainly an extremely valuable way of looking at teaching and learning.

161

INTERVIEW 5: SUSAN MALONEY

*Responses submitted in writing.

RB: Can you introduce yourself briefly?

SM: I am Miss Susan Maloney, a Media and Communications Tutor/ Lecturer at the University of Wollongong, Australia. I began as a Teaching Assistant in Film and Video at the University of California, Santa Cruz, when I was finishing my undergraduate degree. I returned to teaching after a few years of producing and directing corporate video and independent video and television projects. Combined I have almost 17 years university teaching experience.

    I have a strong preference for being behind the camera rather than in front of it but there have been unavoidable times when I have had to step on screen. I have an eclectic dance background (including Hawaiian Hula, Contemporary, Hip Hop, International Folk Dance, African Dance, Flamenco, Salsa, Jazz) and had a short stint teaching dance classes at an adult education institution as well.

RB: In what ways do you see teaching as performance?

SM: As we become more immersed in media and there is increased infusion of media in pedagogy and learning environments, I see a greater emphasis on being engaging and entertaining as well as informed on your topic.

    Learning spaces are far from stoic, quiet halls they may have once been. Academics compete for attention with the laptops and devices that students use.

    I feel that when I stand at the front of a lecture hall or move my way through tutorials, I have to be 'on' and provide as flawless a performance as possible. Our lectures are now recorded for playback, they aren't ephemeral, they are packaged performance pieces. Essentially they double as video on-demand. This creates extra pressure.

    Whether lecturing or tutoring you have to be prepared for questions that have to be answered with speed, wit, and knowledge. The improvisation aspect is not unlike Theatresports. Occasionally a lack of diplomacy or debating skill from the floor is akin to addressing a heckler. If not dealt with successfully, you can lose the whole crowd.

    Also, with the integration of live tweeting in lectures and across the institution, I have to be prepared for further instantaneous comments in the online space as well. There's really no margin for error and it's all in permanent marker.

RB: Do you ever experience stage fright or performance anxiety – on stage and/or in your work as a teacher? If so, how do you manage this?

SM: I experience imposter syndrome and performance anxiety. One strategy I have for reducing this is to never watch a playback of my teaching because I am my own worst critic. I can see why many actors choose not to watch their own movies. For staff training I have had to analyse an example lecture I gave to my peers which was not quite as bad as it felt but my preference remains to not make a regular practice of it. Playback is not nearly as useful as reflecting. I prefer to deliver the content and move on from the performance, rather than replay and ruminate.

I read once that roughly one in five people just won't like you, that doesn't mean they hate you, but they are unlikely to choose the seat beside you at a dinner party or want to invest a single moment into getting to know you. This idea has stayed with me (I wish I still had that article). So I walk into the teaching arena reminding myself that there are potentially one in four people who *will* want to listen and engage with me positively and the one in five who don't or won't do me any harm.

Raising my hands above my head and taking a deep breath when I arrive on campus creates a mini boost in confidence too.

RB: Do you use any of the skills from your work as a performer to enhance your performance in your teaching role? If so, how?

SM: Being mindful of my breathing and how my body is feeling was highly developed through dance. Dance often involves holding a position and then releasing. So when I recognise that I am holding tension in my body, I can locate it and release it almost as a matter of habit. Using the teaching arena like a stage by moving/changing positions while I am lecturing or tutoring is helpful too. How one is using a whole stage is considered when performing, so I think about how I use the whole teaching space. If I notice that students are getting disruptive or chatty I will often stand beside them when I am speaking. Audience focus is similar to a spotlight following me and suddenly they are under it too which helps them to put their own behaviour in check without me having to say something.

RB: To what extent do you think performing arts techniques can help to promote active learning in the classroom?

SM: I think if you possess performing arts skills you already have strategies to draw upon to engage others, to react to surprises and to think on your feet. If for instance the Powerpoint cuts out, you can hold people's attention and continue without access to your teaching aids.

When you dance or perform with others mutual trust is vital. In class I spend a lot of time on icebreaker activities, negotiating expectations, and establishing respect. Underpinning this is the creation of trust amongst students and peers. If you have trust, there is more willingness to be vulnerable, to take risks and to take ownership of the outcomes.

RB: How can an enhanced teaching performance promote inclusivity in learning?

SM: I am not naturally drawn to be in front of others putting on a show, but rather prefer being the one driving it from behind the scenes. So performance, being vulnerable and being 'on' is something I have had to work at. I can relate to students who struggle with having the focus solely on them. I usually set up learning games, presentations and other in-class activities as small group or collective tasks so that each student can grow into different roles without the pressure of feeling unsupported or on show.

I think if you can get everyone in the room active in some way rather than spectating you already have a more inclusive space. You have shared ownership. Each subject is like a production. It may run again but the cast will be different. I put this to my students and ask them to make it as worthwhile as it can be and learn what we can from the whole unique assemblage.

RB: Do you have any top tips for higher education teachers about how they can enhance their performance in the teacher role?

SM: Try to get to know each student's name and one thing about them as you would when working with them on a performance or a production. It charges you with the ability to give on the spot directions and gives you options to involve everyone in some way. Knowing a student's name and being able to call on them tells them that they matter regardless of the perceived size of their role. A sense of interdependence enables your students to contribute, to work with you, and it creates space for them to demonstrate their knowledge and share their skills with greater confidence.

INTERVIEW 6: MARTIN BILLINGHAM

RB: Can you just start by introducing yourself – a bit about your teaching and performance background?

MB: I'm Martin Billingham. I'm a stand-up comedian, I'm an educator and I'm an academic. My personal story is that I always wanted to do stand-up comedy, but I never had the guts. Then I found myself teaching English in Spain and I realised that I was basically doing stand-up comedy: I'm in front of a group of people; I'm interacting with them; I've prepared material that I have to adapt to that particular audience, and I realised: this is stand-up with some of the bits taken off – for a clearly different purpose – obviously you're not trying to get a laugh, but you are trying to elicit a response and then respond to those responses. And that led me down the path of doing a Master's in Stand-up Comedy at the University of Kent. Since then, I have been performing stand-up comedy for seven or eight years now. I've done some work with Stand Up To Cancer, for example. It really strikes me that there's such a connection between the craft of teaching and the craft of the form of public speaking that is stand-up comedy.

RB: That kind of leads into my next question about the links between teaching and performance.

MB: Absolutely. Both through personal experience but also studying it. Much of my career has been as a teaching assistant – I've been in education for nearly 10 years now – and you can tell the difference between a teacher who is willing and able to communicate and one that's not. The classic difference between a bad teacher and a good teacher is a teacher who will stick rigidly to their lesson plan. The big thing about people at the beginning of their teaching experience is that they often cling on to their lesson plan.

RB: I have a question about stage fright, performance anxiety. Is that something you've experienced and, if so, what do you do to try to mitigate the effects of this?

MB: Do I get it? Absolutely! Stand-up comedy is a type of performance where there is no net. Something that's distinct about stand-up comedy compared to other styles of performance is that it's very unscripted. Yes, you have some material and ideas that you've gone through before – before you go up on stage when doing stand-up, it's the worst feeling in the world.

Your body is being surged with adrenaline. Something I tend to do before a gig is I bounce up and down on my toes like a boxer, and that's because I know my body is being flooded with adrenaline and I need to move. The worst thing you can do is sit still and ruminate about the jokes you're about to tell. It's an odd balance because the thing with stand-up comedy is you are writing and editing the show with the audience. But absolutely, before you go on stage, it's the worst feeling in the world; whilst you're doing stand-up, it's the best feeling in the world. And also, when you're more experienced, you crave things going a bit wrong so that you can adapt. So in terms of practical tips: one thing I think – and I tell people who I train – is to just do it! Things are never as bad as you think. Specifically in the teaching context, it's important to make that personal connection with your students; greet them personally at the door. It completely changes the dynamic in the room. Eventually, everyone finds their own way to deal with nerves. They don't go away completely, and they shouldn't go away completely. If you're still nervous – you have butterflies in your stomach – it shows you still care.

Something that's useful about stand-up comedy is realising how you can play with status. I don't mean act – I actually started doing stand-up as a character act, which I scripted, made the costume, everything. But slowly, I got rid of that, realising it was a comfort blanket. And it just got better and better because people want to feel like they connect with the actual individual on stage.

RB: So my next question is about active learning and how your performance skills can help you to create a more active, and interactive, classroom.

MB: I've actually taught professors and lecturers, particularly scientists, about teaching being dialogic. There's a big push towards what's called oracy and dialogic learning. And what they really mean is speaking and listening. The only problem is it's very difficult to assess: we can't see into the minds of our students and they can't see into ours, so that interaction is hard to even see, let alone define, which is what I'm trying to move towards as a researcher and an academic.

Another thing from my point of view as a stand-up comedian is that I'm not trying to make teachers funny. But one thing

stand-up comedians get to do in a clearer way than teachers is
to formatively assess their own communicative ability, and how
their communication is affecting the group in front of them.
With stand-up comedy, it's obvious: you tell a joke, you get a
laugh, so you get an immediate response. And this enables you
to experiment with your persona – the part of you that's public
knowledge. It's a very active way of discovering who you are
in that presentation mode when you're in front of a group and
interacting with them. And that's absolutely useful in terms
of teaching. What is it about you that connects you with other
people? It's as simple as that. Experience in stand-up comedy
is a crash course in that use of status, and being comfortable in your own skin, and use of your persona as a tool for
communication.

RB: And we've spoken a bit about stand-up comedy being quite
unscripted. Can you say a bit about improv techniques you might
use in teaching?

MB: Yes, so the whole point of improv is that you are exercising your
agency not just to perform but also to imagine and to adapt.

Also, do you mean improv or *impro*? Impro is from the British
background and it's really more theatrical.

RB: Is this from Keith Johnstone?

MB: Yes, and *improv* has more of a comedy background and is more
American. Impro in the UK was originally referred to as theatresports. As a practical point for training teachers – one of
the basic concepts in improv is 'yes, and....' This can help with
misbehaviour. So if you get heckled when doing stand-up comedy, it's usually for one of two reasons: either the heckler is drunk
and they just want to be involved, or they're frustrated performers who are not getting the stage time that you've currently got.
The worst thing you can do with a heckler is to absolutely squish
them, because really it's an invitation to play, to be involved.
The best thing to do is to match the level of the heckler. So one
question for you is: why might a teacher use sarcasm in response
to a student?

RB: I guess to deflect the attention back to the student.

MB: Yes, it's doing quite a few things. You're acknowledging and
respecting the student's intelligence, but the sarcasm might
go over the heads of other listeners. And it's similar with a
heckler in stand-up comedy. The worst thing to do is to either

totally ignore it or to be too heavy handed. You want to treat it as if it's an invitation to play, but you are in control of that play. Both the stand-up comedian and the teacher are in constant negotiation with their audience or students as to what happens.

RB: Great, and the last question would be about top tips about performance for HE teachers, but you've kind of given lots throughout. So thank you very much.

INTERVIEW 7: JAMES MARPLES

RB: Can you start by telling us a bit about yourself and your performance background?

JM: Yes, my name is James Marples. I'm a singer-songwriter, composer, and performer. I compose my own music, which is kind of in the Dark Americana genre. I also have a 1950s rock 'n' roll band, from which I make a lot of my living, which plays Elvis, Johnny Cash, and Buddy Holly, and I also compose music for contemporary dance and theatre.

RB: Thank you. Can you say anything about performance and stage fright and what you might do to mitigate the effects of stage fright?

JM: When I was first starting to perform, I used to get lots of stage fright, and I had various practices that I would do. I would sort of work myself up into an excited frenzy beforehand; kind of get myself into a solid state before walking out on stage. Nowadays, I don't really get stage fright. It's more about getting in the moment; feeling like I'm in the moment and connecting with the audience. The way I do that now is I like to go into the room where I'm going to be performing beforehand to suss the room out, figure out where I'm going to be standing, are there any obstructions in my way, how does the seating look like, considering all the practicalities of the room: the acoustics, whether it's dark or light, any possible distractions, and the furniture. I once got a great piece of advice, which is: step 1: take charge of the furniture; set the room up how you want it; say to yourself 'this is my room' and own the teaching or performance space.

RB: So for you, any potential stage fright isn't really about the eyes looking back at you; it's more about things you can control, like the furniture, lights, and so on.

JM: Yeah, when you say 'the eyes looking back at you,' I do still get a bit funny about that, and I still haven't found a way round that even after 17 years or so of performing. I think the way I get round that is I think of myself as performing as a character; a persona. I would feel more nervous thinking of my real-life friends seeing me, the real me, when I'm performing. So I am myself on stage, but I'm a sort of hybrid version of myself. Another thing I do as a performer, and I think is something teachers do too, is utilise whatever is happening in the room at the moment; don't be afraid to use what you're given and go with it.

RB: That's a good lead in to the topic of improvisation. In university teaching, we teach at a high level and at some point, we get questions to which we don't know the answer, so there's an element of improvisation and learning to deal with the unexpected.

JM: Absolutely. And I think teachers and performers have a plan, but the best teachers and performers are able to adapt that plan and react to whatever happens in the room. And the process of planning and preparing is useful, a bit like training a muscle, but then it doesn't matter if you go completely off plan. The fact that you've prepared gives you the confidence to then teach or perform in the moment and to react to events as they unfold.

RB: OK, so perhaps we could talk a bit about performance skills you use in your daily, performing life and to what extent you think any of these skills are applicable to teachers.

JM: So one thing that comes to mind immediately is the ability to throw and vary your voice – especially as a singer. When people describe bad teachers, they often talk about teachers with monotonous voices. So being able to control and vary the dynamics of your voice is a huge part of teaching. In the case of teaching and performance, you're essentially trying to communicate an idea, and a really good teacher and a really good performer brings something out of *you* – it's not about them. And one more thing as a performer is to be aware of any unconscious tics, gestures, or movements that you do that can be distracting to the audience. And I guess that's the same for teachers. So becoming aware of your body and body movements is really important.

RB: OK, and finally, have you got any top tips for higher education teachers from your performance experience?

JM: I feel a bit unqualified to give advice to higher education teachers, but there are some things that I think are useful. One would be what I said earlier – take charge of the furniture, and I mean the whole teaching space and the atmosphere in the space. I think the more you do this, the more it puts you in command of the situation. The second thing I'd say is 'the obstacle is the way.' Use the real, in-the-moment things to your advantage. The things that we see as a problem or a distraction can be turned into something useful. And I think if you think along these lines, you're likely to be less anxious, or have less stage fright, about things potentially going wrong. Those are also the moments that people, or your students, are likely to remember. And the third thing I'd say is to have teaching heroes. This is something performers tend to do naturally – we have heroes who we watch and try to emulate. I guess teachers shouldn't aspire to actually be like someone else, but at least identifying people who inspire you – from a teaching performance perspective – observe them and try to take a little bit of what they have and incorporate it into your own style.

RB: Thank you very much, James.

INTERVIEW 8: MEGAN BYLSMA

*Responses submitted in writing.

RB: Can you introduce yourself briefly?

MB: I am an instructor at Red Deer College in Red Deer, Alberta, Canada. I have been teaching art history survey courses since 2013 and animation history survey since 2018. When I began teaching I had no post-secondary instruction training; I had taught private classes and community classes but had never been at the front of a big auditorium bearing the responsibility of content, testing, and people's possible futures. It was a bit daunting, to say the least. However, I *did* have experience with public speaking and performing. I had grown up in a close-knit church community where sharing personal stories was common and speaking to the congregation was encouraged. I also had been in many music recitals as a musician, had performed on stage as a performance painter as part of my undergraduate Fine Arts degree, and had addressed the student assembly in numerous ways as part of my participation in student politics at college. I have also done voice acting for a colleague who was developing a historical video game.

RB: In what ways do you see teaching as performance?

MB: As Jonté Taylor states, teachers are like stand-up comedians in that the comedian has to be 'responsive to their audiences, and can quickly change things up if they feel that connection slipping. Likewise, good teachers know their students and are able to draw on those relationships to improvise and adapt their teaching in the moment.' (Have a look at: "Why Being a Teacher Is Like Being a Stand-Up Comedian" *ASCD Express*, Vol. 12, No. 13. 2017 http://www.ascd.org/ascd-express/vol12/1213-taylor-2.aspx). A great teacher reads the crowd, knows when to get quiet and draw them, or get loud and get them up and out of their seats. They know when to move towards a noisy table and use their presence as the reminder to pay attention, and when to flail their arms and make horrendous noises as part of their story-lecture to snap that attention back. I think that a teacher who doesn't know that teaching is a performance probably wonders why they aren't an impactful teacher.

I find teaching and performing are incredibly similar in that I have to be present for both. I mean, I can't be locked up in my head, wondering how things are going, concerned if the tea stain on my shirt is noticeable still, and hoping that I didn't offend my colleague in the hall. All those thoughts and worries have to be pushed aside and the only thing in my moment has to be what I need to say or do and the students in front of me. The best teaching moments are when everything else falls away and it's just me, my students, and the story of history I'm talking about, modelling, or getting them to interact with. A good performance follows similar paths, I think. I can't sing all that well if I'm worried about the fact that I don't like my earrings. I have to be *consumed* by the song and have it and its communication as the only thing I focus on.

I teach the history of art. It's basically the best topic to teach because it's stories with illustrations. It's a gimme as far as impactful content and teaching is concerned. And it also means I get this great opportunity to teach by using humanity's most powerful tool – the story. One of my favourite classes is when, in my introductory course, we talk about Vincent Van Gogh. Everyone knows who this guy is, and everybody is interested in this tortured genius, and everyone brings some kind of knowledge to that class already. And this creates a perfect opportunity to dive into some deep learning and perspective shifting information through telling a story. In that class I have to consciously take on the role of a master storyteller. I have to make sure I'm present, I'm aware, and I'm firmly rooted in my body – using every gesture and every step around the room as part of the story I weave. A story of a troubled man's desire to be liked, to find purpose, to help others, and to never let anyone down. The story of a man who takes the blame for other's actions and is highly influenced by the stimulus around him. A man who, perhaps, has more to offer us than a caricature of mental illness. A man who never knew he was going to be the world's most famous artist as he never sold a painting in his entire life time and the one that he may have sold was likely purchased by an art school to show students how *not* to paint. In that class, when the story is told right, 100 students gasp together, laugh together, and are silent together. When the performance of teaching that class is done well students never forget Vincent Van Gogh and how the story of his life is a dreadful reminder about how much Western society likes to engage with stereotype but is reluctant to engage with real humanity and emotion.

RB: Do you ever experience stage fright or performance anxiety – on stage and/or in your work as a teacher? If so, how do you manage this?

MB: Yes! The first class I ever taught I was a shaky and butter-fly-filled mess. Until I stepped up to the podium and started to teach. Being present meant I had to admit I was nervous, so nervous, and then let it go by immersing myself in connecting with my students and the content I was delivering to them. I still get performance anxiety before new classes sometimes. But now I don't feel I have to hide it like I did when I was a brand new teacher. Now I stop, tell my students, "Wow! I'm really nervous for some reason guys! I think I'm really afraid I'm going to mess this year up. But that makes no sense! I've done this before and this is going to be *great!*" Sharing vulnerability with students can be a powerful teaching tool, especially if I use it to model resilience and working through anxiety.

I actually find performance anxiety before a musical perfor-mance much harder to shake off than public speaking fright. But I believe the reason for that is that I *have* to follow what the music says – there's no chance to pace the delivery in the way that I have control over a lesson – and shaking hands and voice are super unhelpful to playing an instrument and singing. So the more I try not to be nervous and shaky the less I inhabit my body and the more I get tangled in my mind and…the more my voice and hands shake.

However, whether it's being nervous before a class (sometimes if I have controversial topics that are on the agenda I also get nervous before that class) or nervous before performing, I find the bigger the pre-fright, the bigger the post-high. After-performance highs are the payoff for being scared beforehand. And the biggest thing I have to remember when I get a case of the nerves is the things I learned from improv theatre: laughter signals to the audience you are okay if you mess up and this makes it okay for them to feel okay too, make the audience your friend and they'll root for you even if things aren't perfect, and make the audience comfortable and you won't have to fight them for a good performance.

RB: Do you use any of the skills from your work as a performer to enhance your performance in your teaching role? If so, how?

MB: Every day! Voice modulation is a secret weapon. As a female instructor I have to be careful with my intonation as female instructors (or speakers of any kind) are very easy to criticise as being 'shrill' and a shrill speaker is one that society has given permission to dismiss without listening to. I also have a fairly high natural voice, so I need to be careful – especially when tired or stressed – that it doesn't get screechy. Which means I often use my 'recording' voice – which is still me, just a bit more modulated, slightly more 'sweet' sounding, and a whole lot louder. And changing voices to express things is *highly* effective; especially when I want to signal to my students that this story is meant to connect with them, meant to make them laugh, meant to make them consider. There's nothing that signals snooty, upper-class bias like switching to an (albeit pretty bad) "Mid-Atlantic" accent, while signalling boorish outrage to some development in the art world is easily done by switching to some facsimile of a Midwestern hick from a John Wayne movie, or putting some Maritime twang and an 'eh' at the end of every sentence gives a good impression of the general Canadian response to something. It's a risk working with voice changes, noticeable intonation, etc. but I've found that taking the risk is like practice – the more I do it the easier and more versatile it becomes. Sometimes if I mess it up there's the chance to have a do-over. Literally stopping the lecture/story and saying "oh wait. I can do that better." And then

173

re-voicing the statement. Other times it's clearly not appropriate timing to get a re-take so I have to live with having let loose a weird way of talking that wasn't quite anything but strange for a sentence or two. In terms of social risk it's not a giant risk, but it sometimes seems like it is a huge social risk when I know playing with some voices could be helpful but I'm too chicken to try.

I purposely use my body in my lecture. I am a wandering lecturer anyway, so I try to use the motions of my body to express the enthusiasm I have for my content. My classes are generally three hours long at a time, so it makes for an exhausting physical exercise to pace, wave my arms, dance on the spot, jump up and down, or whatever the lesson and my students end up requiring. Some years students don't really need a lot of body-activity from me to be engaged. Other years I practically do an interpretive dance with every lecture to keep their heads above the waters of boredom.

Answering questions on the fly. This is an instructional technique that seems to rarely be addressed but came up a lot when I was mentoring new teachers. The answer to building that skill, I've found, is in working on my improv skills. A great improv-er isn't locked in their head, and isn't looking to reach a preconceived conclusion. They're present in their body and working with those around them to find a community-based conclusion. Answering unexpected questions (that really can come out of nowhere, can test the edges of my knowledge, and sometimes seem to be tied to the present topic in only the most tenuous ways) really requires that same 'Yes, and' attitude that an improv actor has. Sometimes being willing to be wrong (which is how teachers feel about saying "I don't know") and willing to say "That's a good question. I'm going to find out." or "Let's look that up!" is what is needed and is part of the ability to take risks that improv hones. But being able to roll with those questions is only really possible when I'm rooted in the moment, but not just the moment, but also the group and their connection to me.

I once had a class (that was being observed by a colleague for my performance review, of course) that had an outbreak of unexpected questions. We had been learning about cathedrals and relics and my students became fixated on the fact that glass is a semi-viscous solid – as time passes the glass at the bottom of the pane becomes thicker as the glass at the top becomes impossibly thin – in relation to stain glass windows. This fascinated them and in the middle of a lecture about architecture I started fielding questions about the physics of the existence of glass, its upkeep, and its conservation. Talking about the fragile nature of old glass, its reaction to heat and flame, and how much longer very old stain glass would continue to hold up was *not* where my lecture was supposed to go, but that's where we went. The answers to these questions were not in my notes or in the text. This was very much on-the-fly and depended on my ability to apply knowledge across disciplines. But we rolled with it and eventually got back on track. Not twenty minutes later as I was discussing Roman Catholic relics, I showed a non-religious scientific 'relic' in the form of Galileo's mummified middle finger. The ghoulish story of how he had been exhumed and reburied and how a grave digger had stolen Galileo's finger and how it was some kind of amusing irony that it ended up being his middle finger was all part of my lecture. What wasn't part of my lecture was the barrage of questions regarding how he became mummified and a mini side-lecture regarding the conditions required for human mummification and Roman Catholic sanctions regarding the moving and removal of bodies, and parts thereof, in the 1700s. Thank goodness for a long history of watching *CSI* and *Bones* and an undergrad paper regarding the Incans making it possible for me to cover the basics of natural mummification, because let me tell you, the answers to those questions were *not* in the text! Because I was loose and just in the flow of the class, and not hung up on the flow of my lecture, I was able to incorporate these discussions into my class and not horrify my observer too much with the macabre fascinations of my students.

RB: To what extent do you think performing arts techniques can help to promote active learning in the classroom?

MB: In my second level classes I use a pedagogy called Reacting to the Past. It's a curriculum that was developed to make history come alive to students. The modules I have used always relate to historical art events, but the way this curriculum works is that students are assigned research topics that revolve around real people from history, all their writing over the course of the term is about this person they've been assigned, and then when we reach the point that we start to dig into that time period (everyone is assigned humans from the same time period and geographical place) the students *become* those people from history and interact in class as those historical figures. It's not a re-enactment, but a reacting to the social pressures and events of the time and the students try to make decisions, build relationships, and persuade each other based on and from the perspective of the beliefs and values of the person they were assigned. Essentially it's a very carefully constructed role-playing game. Students become the leaders in the class and they apply their knowledge as deeply as they can. It's a very active classroom experience, as students are the leaders in the classroom and for the few weeks that we run through this immersion scenario there are no lectures and no teacher – the teacher becomes the 'GM' who is there to help with snags, offer advice when asked, help with strategizing plans, and to give a gentle nudge to anyone who might be freezing up a bit.

This kind of classroom experience is chaotic for many as there is no precedent for what is successful and what is not from the student's perspective. Students have to take risks. But students can only take those risks and be active in the classroom when they know the teacher has their back. When they know that the teacher has been taking risks, that the teacher understands that not all gambles pay out the way we hope, and that the point isn't the specific pre-planned answer at the end but the ways a person can say 'Yes, and' to get to the end of the journey and then examine all the things we've picked up on the way. To build a classroom where this kind of active learning takes place requires the teacher to have confidence that even if mistakes are made, they can be addressed at the end of the 'performance' and set right then. And it also requires a teacher who has prepared their students to feel safe taking such risks with their learning and, in the students' minds, their grades. Creating that safety and trust is best done, in my experience, through team-building exercises that are rooted in an improv methodology. Setting students up for success, in my opinion, often requires they learn the basic ideas and tools of an improv troupe. If they can be silly, learn to have a 'Yes, and' attitude with each other, and know that whatever they say as their historical character won't be used against them as their student selves can create an environment where experiential, active, and enjoyable learning takes place.

RB: How can an enhanced teaching performance promote inclusivity in learning?

MB: The Reacting to the Past pedagogy that I talked about before is definitely something that can work in this way. I have had students remark that after the Reacting module finished, they 'felt' about historical figures and understood their humanity in their decisions, even if the student didn't agree with them. And this has spilled over, from my observation, to dealing with their colleagues. I don't believe it was that the empathy they practised in their research and class interactions with history that created the empathy with their peers though – I feel that empathy is a skill that can be honed, but it takes time and patience. I believe their new-found patience and kindness with each other stems from the bonding that occurs when people encourage each other, work together, and start to interact with each other in unexpected ways. It builds relationships and creates a unity that sitting in a lecture class definitely does not.

In my lower level classes I've started working in improv exercises for the students as well in an effort to build that rapport between students. It can definitely work to diminish the number of inter-student squabbles I need to deal with.

RB: Do you have any top tips for higher education teachers about how they can enhance their performance in the teacher role?

MB: Get out of your head! Academics seem to be locked up in their minds, always judging, critiquing, and evaluating. That's part of the job. But to be a great teacher you have to let that go, turn it off, and just move like water with the flow. Save the self-reflection and critique for after the last student leaves the room and then reflect on what was good and what wasn't. But doing that reflection while you're teaching is going to freeze you up. And not doing that reflection ever is going to make it so you don't realize your students are in a boredom coma.

Come to terms with the fact that each class is a performance. Higher education teachers could hate this concept as it seems to imply 'edutainment' instead of education. However, instead see it as something that is already part of your role whether you like it or not and something you can get better at. Performers know that practice and trying out new things is the way to gain great performances. And sometimes a performance is really not good, but that's just fuel to feed your next performance to make it so much better.

My biggest tip is to read *Teach Like a PIRATE: Increase Student Engagement, Boost Your Creativity, and Transform Your Life as an Educator* by Dave Burgess. It might not be directed at higher education professionals, but it can sure apply to our job. And it will definitely make you see your job as a performer/educator as something that can be amazing.

INTERVIEW 9: ANNA MCNAMARA

RB: Can you start by telling us a bit about yourself and your performance background?

AM: I trained at GSA in the late 90s and then completed an MA in Education. I've been a teacher ever since. I joined the GSA faculty in January 2012 and am now the school's Director of Learning and Teaching.

RB: To what extent are teaching and performance linked?

AM: In so many ways! Students can in some ways be considered our audience, but in a more active, participatory way than an audience watching a performance. The lecture is the obvious format that highlights the link between teaching and performance. We just have to think about the lecture hall as an auditorium. There is an oratory tradition to these spaces, but the Greeks referred to the stage as the orchestra which means the dancing place. Nowadays, lectures also add a huge screen and project presentation slides, so our students are sitting in a kind of cinema. This can, perhaps inevitably, build a sense of expectation of the lecturer to fulfil the role of performer. Some in this position don't have the skills or training to gain and keep students' attention. Voice is an important tool in doing this – projecting the voice, varying the intonation and volume of the voice, communicating a message and telling an engaging story, safely, and healthily. Also vital is keeping the critical eye at bay – the lecturer must stay in communication with their audience, without critiquing or commenting on their own delivery, as this serves to undermine their confidence and authenticity.

RB: And can I ask about the skills you might learn from performance and how these might be applied to teaching?

AM: There are so many. Correct breathing is really important. Centring and grounding your breathing and your physicality in the space can help you to communicate in a calm and assured way. I think it's also really important to be honest, authentic and to work in the moment. I don't like the idea of academics as gurus who have all the answers to students' questions. I am always very honest with my students and I tell them if I don't know the answer to something, and then we can co-construct the learning together. This is why I think it's more helpful to think about the students as the performers, or better, as the storytellers. The lecturer on the stage cannot be the focus of the lesson. The students as co-constructors of stories must be in the 'dancing place.'

RB: That's interesting because I often advise teachers to record themselves – perhaps in a microteaching session – in order to become more aware of how they look, sound...

AM: Yes, and that can be very useful. But we also have to be aware that actors are trained to act in front of a camera, because it's not natural to just 'continue as normal' with a camera pointing at you. So there is a question about whether a teacher will be 'performing' authentically as soon as a camera is there.

RB: Thank you. I also have a question about the important issues of inclusivity and active learning in higher education. How do you think an enhanced teaching performance can help to make learning more active and promote inclusivity?

AM: I think it's all about telling stories. Whatever we do, the human experience is about telling stories – our own stories, others' stories. And that's what researchers, lecturers, and academics do essentially. They tell stories about their research. Storytelling is the basic communication skill of a good teacher – or performer. If you can do this, you will be able to engage students in an active learning process. You will also be able to empathise with different people's stories and backgrounds, which enables you to design more inclusive learning experiences for your students. We have to think of ourselves as storytellers working with students who are also storytellers. They are not to be considered our audience, or consumers passively receiving a product. They're right in the narrative with us.

RB: And finally, do you have any top tips for higher education teachers about how they can enhance their performance?

AM: Yes, I think as I've said before, being honest and authentic is key. So you're not really acting; you're being yourself. I talk a lot about the connection between thought, feeling and action. We cannot deliver anything in life authentically without these three elements being connected and in tune. We think, we feel, we do.

And the other thing I've mentioned already is storytelling: if you can develop your ability to tell stories, you will be able to engage your learners in active, collaborative learning. What does any good performer, teacher, author do? They communicate messages by telling good stories.

RB: Thank you very much.

179

INTERVIEW 10: CLARE CHANDLER

RB: Can you just start with a brief introduction to who you are, your teaching, your performance background?

CC: I'm a Senior Lecturer in Musical Theatre and in that capacity I teach across musical theatre practice, so acting technique, vocal technique, critical analysis, engagement with critical theory, and so on. I've taught in a variety of contexts. Most recently I've taught in higher education and I've taught in that vein at the City of Liverpool College, at LIPA, at Edge Hill where I am currently and at Wolverhampton, where I will be from September 2019. Then my background as a performer is similarly eclectic: I've worked as a singer, as an actress, as a musician, in a variety of different genres and practice – Shakespeare, musical theatre, supporting Ringo Starr – so all of this experience is now inter-woven into my teaching practice. I think also as a teacher, or a tutor or a lecturer – and I think the language people use to define themselves is quite interesting – I've got quite a varied background as well. I've worked as a workshop facilitator with NEETs (not in education, employment, or training), young adults with disabilities, so I've got quite a broad spectrum of experience, which also feeds into my teaching practice. And I think my teaching is definitely enhanced by my performing experience.

RB: Thank you. That leads on well to the next question about the extent to which teaching and performance are linked.

CC: I think they're intrinsically linked. If we take the most basic definition of performance – it's live and it has an audience – you have your empty space and your audience – let's go back to Brook. And similarly with teaching, the audience being your students. Also in terms of Fischer-Lichte and this notion of autopoiesis, so this cycle of energy and engagement is something that's present within the classroom or the lecture in that there's this cycle of energy and knowledge between the student and the teacher. And as such, as the teacher or the performer, you need to be conscious of that engagement. You're presenting knowledge in a performative manner in order to facilitate understanding. So your teaching, your performance, your practice needs to be reactive and responsive to what's happening in the room. We've all had sessions where you've planned it, you go in and think it's going to be amazing, but for whatever reasons it isn't working and you have to change and adapt in order to meet the audience or get them to meet you. So this relationship between student and teacher is integral to ideas that link teaching and performance.

RB: So my next question is about stage fright, performance anxiety and the extent to which you've experienced this.

CC: I suppose I'm lucky in that I've never experienced any horrendously paralysing stage fright or performance anxiety. I think there's always something there, isn't there, like a nervous energy before doing a new show or revisiting something after a long time. And similarly as an educator, there's a nervous energy perhaps before teaching a group you've not taught before. So there's that same feeling of nerves or anticipation. There's that potential for mishaps and this notion of liveness; that things could and will go wrong. But this nervous energy propels you through this. In terms of how I manage it, I go back to what I would do as a performer, so preparation, breathing, use your pre-show or pre-teaching rituals, whatever they might be, so perhaps warm-ups, going over my script or notes, making sure I'm aware of the performance space or classroom, doing a tech rehearsal, and making sure everything is working. And then being mindful within the performance or during teaching of how nerves can impact upon delivery, so ensuring I'm not rushing through material, or that my diction isn't going – so being mindful of myself in the moment.

RB: Thank you. So you've already spoken a bit about this, but perhaps you could talk some more about skills and techniques from performance that you bring into your teaching.

CC: I think things like diction and articulation and an awareness of the need to warm yourself up vocally. Teachers can experience lots of vocal issues because of misusing their instrument. Performers spend lots of time on vocal training and yet within teaching practice, you rarely find sessions in teacher training on vocal health. I think it's also important to be able to read the room and respond in the moment. Another thing is awareness of body language, both mine and the students, because often nerves will lead to withdrawn, closed body language. Also an awareness of flow and energy. So if you race through a monologue, it's not going to have much impact. And you can apply that to teaching as well, such as knowing the peaks and troughs, the suspension and release. I've also thought about heckling. So in a performance context, you might have engagement from the audience that you don't necessarily want. For example, I was playing Mrs Twit in a production of *The Twits*, and Mr Twit and I were encouraging rebellion from the audience, but then it was difficult to bring them back so that the piece could continue. And it's the same in teaching. Sometimes students might ask questions that you haven't planned for and they might not respond in the way you expected. I've seen colleagues without a performance background fearful of this, whereas training in performance and improvisation perhaps enables you to follow the flow of their thoughts as opposed to shutting down interactions where students aren't following as expected.

RB: That makes me think of status – something I discussed in one of the other interviews.

CC: Definitely. Status is really interesting because it's how within that relationship you perform the status. I remember watching a colleague leading a seminar and she was sat on a chair and the university students were sitting on the floor around her. I always try to sit on the same level as the students. Also I think the use of humour and status is important. So, for example, students might be playing on their phones, and it's about how you manage that. And you can do that with humour in a way that doesn't make people feel small or stupid but it clearly outlines what you expect. This ties into notions of etiquette in the theatre or classroom. I saw a performance of *The Nico Project* with Maxine Peake, and a man, at quite an intense moment, got up to go to the toilet. You really felt sorry for him because it was embarrassing for him. And the actress, Peake, acknowledged it. It just so happened that the line was about leaving, so she just looked at the man and raised an eyebrow. So it's about knowing when you can disrupt your script to acknowledge what's going on in the room. What else? Breathing and breath control. Space – not being afraid of silence.

RB: Great, you've said lots there. Is there anything else about performance that helps particularly in engaging students actively in their learning?

CC: Well, because of all those different elements going on in performance, we have quite short attention spans, so I tend to try and engage students in quite short and focused tasks. I'm mindful of my experience as a performer – that when you give an audience too much space, they don't always go where you want them to go. So keeping students engaged through varied questioning techniques. And if you're uncertain about things, acknowledge the uncertainty but not in a way that's apologetic. Make it more collaborative. Active learning is about being in charge of the space and the pace; being conscious that if energy is dwindling, knowing what else you can do or how you can motivate the students on to whatever the next task is. I think as well especially in the consumerist environment we're in now, students want to know that the person standing in front of them knows what they're talking about. So there has to be an element of presenting yourself, and any uncertainty about activities that you're trying out, in a positive way, and not making them feel like you're experimenting on them.

RB: And the final question is about inclusivity and how being a performer can help you to make your teaching more inclusive.

CC: There's an element of empathy as a performer because you need to be able to get into the heads of your characters or personas that you're creating. So that would feed into this idea of inclusivity in learning and teaching. And also to find a shared horizon of expectations between myself and my students, so as the gap between myself and them becomes greater – as time goes on, you don't have the same cultural references anymore – you need to find other shared references. It's also about considering that there is lots of individuality in the room and how you can address those differences whilst playing your part. This isn't something that I feel my performance experience has fed into necessarily, but maybe that's because I hadn't considered it before.

RB: OK, thank you. Is there anything in summary that you would say in terms of top tips for teachers from your performance experience?

CC: Yes, so preparation, practice, consideration of this idea of flow of energy, and information. Being reactive and reflective in your practice, and humour. Also this consideration of status. When I observe some colleagues, they are sometimes limiting what they want to achieve because they play or enforce a status relationship that the students don't believe, so they inadvertently undermine themselves. As a performer, you are perhaps more aware of how you maintain a role consistently. There has to be an element of trust in the performer, or in the lecturer. I see colleagues who are desperate to be liked – and it's the same with some performers. And that can be quite damaging, so it's about how to find a way that works for you but also how to some extent become immune to the need for such reinforcement from your students.

RB: That's great, thank you very much.

Index

Note: **Bold** page numbers refer to tables.